James Grant

Second to None

A Military Romance Vol. 1

James Grant

Second to None
A Military Romance Vol. 1

ISBN/EAN: 9783744776189

Printed in Europe, USA, Canada, Australia, Japan

Cover: Foto ©Thomas Meinert / pixelio.de

More available books at **www.hansebooks.com**

SECOND TO NONE.

A Military Romance.

BY

JAMES GRANT,

AUTHOR OF
"THE ROMANCE OF WAR," "THE CAPTAIN OF THE GUARD,"
"THE YELLOW FRIGATE," ETC. ETC.

IN THREE VOLUMES.

VOL. I.

LONDON:
ROUTLEDGE, WARNE, AND ROUTLEDGE,
BROADWAY, LUDGATE HILL.
NEW YORK: 129, GRAND STREET.
1864.

PREFACE.

In the following pages, and in delineating the character of my hero, I have chosen the ranks of the 2nd Dragoons, not because of any national partiality, but from the desire to describe the adventures of a soldier in a brave old regiment, which has served with distinction in every war since its formation—in short, from the battles of the Covenant to those in the Crimea; which had the proud distinction of capturing the Colours of the Regiment du Roi at Ramillies, the White Standard of King Louis' Household Troops at Dettingen, and the Colour and Eagle of Napoleon's 45th Foot at Waterloo.

Several historical incidents, and one or two traditions of the Service are interwoven with the story of Basil Gauntlet, the Scots Grey.

I may mention that the misfortunes of his comrade Charters are nearly similar to those which befel an officer of the 15th Hussars prior to the war in the Peninsula; and that the dark story and death of the engineer Monjoy and of Madame d'Escombas formed one of the *causes célèbres* before the Parliament of Paris during the middle of the last century.

EDINBURGH, 1st *May*, 1864.

CONTENTS

OF

THE FIRST VOLUME.

SECOND TO NONE.

CHAPTER I.

BY THE WAYSIDE.

My adventures were my sole inheritance long before I thought of committing them to paper for the amusement of myself, and—may I hope—for the instruction of others.

Wayward has been my fate—my story strange; for my path in life—one portion of it at least—has been among perils and pitfalls, and full of sorrow and mortification, but not, however, without occasional gleams of sunshine and triumph.

On an evening in the month of February—no matter in what year, suffice it to say that it was long, long ago—I found myself near a little town on the Borders between England and Scotland, with a shilling in my hand, and this small coin I surveyed with certain emotions of solicitude, because it was my *last one*.

I sat by the wayside under an old thorn-tree whereon the barons of Netherwood had hung many a Border outlaw and English mosstrooper in the olden time; and there I strove to consider what I should do next; but my mind seemed a very chaos.

In this unenviable condition I found myself on the birthday of my eighteenth year—I, the heir to an old title and to a splendid fortune—homeless, and well-nigh penniless, without having committed a crime or an error of which conscience could accuse me.

The rolling clouds were gathering in grey masses on the darkening summits of the Cheviot hills in the hollows of which the snows of the past winter lay yet unmelted. The cold wind moaned in the leafless woods, and rustled the withered leaves that the autumn gales had strewn along the highway. The dull February evening crept on, and the road that wound over the uplands was deserted, for the last wayfarer had gone to his home. The sheep were in their pen and the cattle in their fold; no sound—not even the bark of a dog—came from the brown sides of the silent hills, and, affected by the gloomy aspect of Nature, my heart grew heavy, after its sterner and fiercer emotions passed away.

The last flush of sunset was fading in

the west; but I could see about three miles distant the gilt vanes and round turrets of Netherwood Hall shining above the grove of leafless trees that surrounded it, and I turned away with a sigh of bitterness, for adversity had not yet taught me philosophy. I was too young.

With the express intention of visiting Netherwood Hall, I had travelled several miles on foot; but now, when in sight of the place, my spirit failed and my heart sickened within me; and thus, irresolute and weary, I seated myself by the side of the way, and strove to arrange my thoughts.

To be brief, I shall describe in a few pages, who and what I am, and how on that sombre February evening I came to be on such unfortunate terms with old Dame Fortune.

My grandfather, Sir Basil Gauntlet, of

Netherwood, had so greatly resented his eldest son's marriage with a lady who had no fortune save her beauty, that he withdrew all countenance and protection from him. So far did he carry this unnatural enmity, that by will he bequeathed all his property to the son of a brother, and, with great barbarity, permitted my father to be consigned to the King's Bench prison, by which his commission in the cavalry was forfeited; and there, though a brave and high-spirited officer, who had served under the Marquis of Granby, he died of despair!

My mother soon followed him to the land that lies beyond the grave; and thus in infancy I was left, as the phrase is, to the *tender* mercies of the world in general, and my old bruin of a grandfather in particular.

Yet this upright Sir Basil, who was so

indignant at his son's penniless marriage, had been in youth one of the wildest rakes of his time. He had squandered vast sums on the lovely Lavinia Fenton—the original Polly Peachum—and other fair dames, her contemporaries; indeed, it was current in every green-room in London, that he would have run off with this beautiful actress, had he not been anticipated, as all the world knows, or ought to know, by his grace the Duke of Bolton, who made her his wife.

Sir Basil had been wont to drink his three bottles daily, as he said, "without a hair of his coat being turned." He had paraded three of his best friends, on three different occasions, for over-night insults of which he had a very vague recollection in the morning; but then "after what had occurred," what else could he do? and so after bathing his head and right arm in vinegar to make his aim steady, he winged them all at Wimbledon Common, or the back of Montagu House.

In London he was the terror of the watch, and would smash all the lamps in Pall Mall or elsewhere, when, after losing perhaps a thousand guineas at White's among blacklegs and bullies, or after carrying the sedan of some berouged fair one through the streets with links flaring before it, he came reeling home, probably with a broken sword in one hand, a bottle in the other, and his pockets stuffed with brass knockers and other men's wigs; consequently Sir Basil should have remembered the days of his youth, and have tempered the acts of his old age with mercy; but it was otherwise.

I do not mean to detain the reader by a long history of my earlier years; for if those of a Cæsar or an Alexander have but little in them to excite interest, still less must the boyhood of one who began the world as a simple dragoon in the king's service.

The good minister of Netherwood, and the English rector on the south side of the Border, frequently besought Sir Basil to be merciful to the orphan child of his eldest son.

"I pray you to recollect, Sir Basil," urged the rosy-faced rector, "that your own marriage was a love-match."

"It must have been so, if all you scandalous fellows at Oxford said truth."

"Why?"

"For there you said I loved the whole female sex."

The jolly rector laughed so much at the poor jest of the old rake, that the latter actually became commiserate; or it may be that my mother's death and my utter desolation, stirred some emotion of shame—pity he had none—in Sir Basil's arid heart; so, to keep me at a distance from himself, he consigned me on a pittance to the care of his country agent, a certain Mr. Nathan Wylie, who was exceedingly well-named, as he was a canting Scotch lawyer — in truth "a cunning wretch whose shrivelled heart was dead to every human feeling," and who by the sharpness of his legal practice was a greater terror on both sides of the Border than ever the mosstroopers were of old.

He was the person who had prepared and executed the will which transferred my heritage to my cousin, Tony Gauntlet —a will which he framed with peculiar satisfaction, as he hated my father for making free with his orchard in boyhood, and in later years for laying a horsewhip across his shoulders at the market-cross of Greenlaw, so in his sanctified dwelling I was likely to have a fine time of it!

For ten years I resided with the godly Nathan Wylie, a repining drudge, ill-fed, ill-clad, and poorly lodged, in one of those attics which he apportioned to Abraham Clod, his groom, his pigeons and myself—uncared for by all; and not unfrequently taunted with the misfortunes of my parents for whom I sorrowed, and the neglect of my grandfather whom I had learned to abhor and regard with boyish terror.

I picked up a little knowledge of law—at least such knowledge as one might learn in the office of a Scotch country agent in those days. I mastered, I believe, even "Dirlton's Doubts," and other equally amusing literature then in vogue; while Nathan Wylie took especial care that I should know all the shorter catechism, and other biblical questions by rote, that I might be able to repeat them when the minister paid us his periodical visit, though my elbows were threadbare, my shoes none of the best, and my eyes and brain ached with drudging at the desk far into the hours of the silent night, penning prosy documents, preparing endless processes, and not unfrequently writing to dictation such an epistle as the following, which I give *verbatim* as it actually appeared in a Border paper :—

"DEAR SIR,—I am directed to raise an action against you to-morrow for the sum of one penny, together with the additional sum of three shillings and fourpence, sterling, the expense of this notice, if both sums be not paid me before 9 a.m.

"Yours, faithfully in the Lord,

"NATHAN WYLIE.

"To Farmer Flail, &c."

In early life he had married an old and equally devout female client for the money which he knew well she possessed; and as that was all he wanted, after her death he never married again, but devoted himself manfully to the practice of the law and extempore prayer—an external air of great sanctity being rather conducive to success in life in too many parts of Scotland.

Poor Nathan has long been laid six feet under the ground; but in fancy I can still see before me his thin figure, with rusty black suit and spotless white cravat; his sharp visage, with keen, restless, and cat-like eyes, that peered through a pair of horn spectacles, and with shaggy brows that met above them. Moreover, he had hollow temples, coarse ears, and a tiger-like jaw, which he always scratched vigorously when a case perplexed him, or with satisfaction when some hapless client was floored in the field of legal strife.

As years stole on, that keen and honest sense of justice, which a boy seldom fails to feel, inspired me with indignation at the neglect with which my family treated me, and the story of my parents and their fate redoubled my hatred to my oppressors.

My cousin Tony, a harebrained fool, whose mad fox-hunting adventures formed the theme of all the Border side, and who, by my grandfather's lavish and misplaced generosity, was enabled to pursue a career of prodigality and extravagance, came in for a full share of my animosity, for he was wont to ride past me on the highway without the slightest recognition, save once, when, flushed with wine, he was returning from a hunting-dinner.

On that occasion he was ungenerous

enough to draw the attention of his groom and whipper-in to the somewhat dilapidated state of my attire, as I was trudging along the highway on some legal message to Farmer Flail at the Woodland Grange.

On hearing their derisive laughter, my heart swelled with suppressed passion, and had a weapon been in my hand, I had struck them all from their saddles.

This crushing existence was not the glorious destiny my boyish ambition had pictured; but what could I do for a time, save submit? I had none to guide me—nor father, nor mother, nor kindred were there; and as a child, I often gazed wistfully at other children who *had* all these, and marvelled in my lonely heart what manner of love they had for one another.

I was conscious of possessing a fund of affection, of kindness and goodwill in my own bosom; but there it remained pent up for lack of an object whereon to lavish it, or rather it was thrust back upon me by the repulsive people by whom I was surrounded.

Business over, I would rush away to solitude. Sunk in reveries, vague and deep, I would stroll for hours alone in the starlight along the green and shady lanes, or by the silent shore, where the German sea rolled its creamy waves in ceaseless and monotonous succession on the shingles, or from whence it rippled in the splendour of the moonlight far away—reveries filled less with vain regrets than with visions of a brilliant future, for my heart was young, inspired by hope and thoughts that soared above my present condition, and sought a brighter destiny!

I could remember a time—alas! it seemed a dream to me now—when I used to repose in a pretty little bed, and when a lady, who must have been my mother, pale and thin and gentle-eyed, and richly-attired too, for her satin dress rustled, and her presence had a sense of perfume, was wont to draw back the curtains of silk and white lace to caress and to kiss me. Once a tear fell on my cheek—it was hot—and she brushed it aside with a tress of her gathered hair.

Was all this a reality, or a dream? I strove to conjure up when and where I had seen this; but the memory of it was wavering, and so indistinct, that at times the treasured episode seemed to fade away altogether.

In the long nights of winter I saved up my candles—no easy task in the house of a miser like Nathan Wylie—and, retreating to my attic, read far into the hours of morning; poring over such novels and romances as were lent me by the village milliner, a somewhat romantic old maiden, who had been jilted by a recruiting officer, and for whose memory she always shed a scanty tear, for he fell at the bombardment of Carthagena. These books I read by stealth, such literature being deemed trash and dangerous profanity in the godly mansion of Nathan Wylie.

Then when the wind, that tore down the rocky ravines of the Cheviots, howled in the chimneys, or shook the rafters above me, I loved to fancy myself at sea, for the life of a sailor seemed to embody all my ideas of perfect freedom—a bold buccaneer, like Sir Henry Morgan—a voyager, like Drake or Dampier—a conqueror, like Hawke or Boscawen—a wanderer, like dear old Robinson Crusoe, or worthy Philip Quarll; and then I went to sleep and to dream of foreign lands, of lovely isles full of strange trees and wondrous flowers, where scaly serpents crawled, and spotted tigers lurked; of cities that were all bannered towers, gilded cupolas and marble temples, glittering in the sunshine far beyond the sea.

A lonely child, I ripened into a lonely lad, and so passed my life, until the coming of Ruth Wylie, an event which fully deserves a chapter to itself.

CHAPTER II.

RUTH WYLIE.

Love occasioned my first scrape in life, and thus it came to pass.

About the period of my aimless existence, detailed in the last chapter, the mansion of Mr. Nathan Wylie received a new, and to him, in no way welcome inmate, in the person of an orphan niece from London, the daughter of a brother who had died in circumstances the reverse of affluent, bequeathing this daughter—then in her sixteenth year—to his care.

This brother's letter—one penned on his death-bed in an agony of anxiety for the *future* of his orphan Ruth—was deeply touching in its simple tenor; and some of the references therein to years that had long passed away, and to the pleasant days of their boyhood, should have been more than enough to soften even the heart of Nathan Wylie; but he read it unmoved, with a grimace on his thin mouth and his beetle brows knit.

Then he carefully folded and docketed it among others, with a gleam of irritation in his cat-like eyes; and equally unmoved by sympathy or compassion did he receive his charge, when she arrived by the stage-coach from London, pale with sorrow, weary with travel, and clad in cheap and simple mourning for the father she had lost.

One generally imagines a Ruth to be solemn, demure, and quiet—something between a little nun and a Quakeress; but Ruth Wylie sorely belied her name, being a merry, kind, and affectionate girl, with bewitching dark eyes, full of fun and waggery, especially when uncle Nathan was absent, for she failed to conceal that his hard, short, and dry manner, and his cold, immoveable visage chilled and saddened her.

New and strange thoughts came into my mind now; and soon I conceived a regard for Ruth, notwithstanding her hideous relation, the lawyer; for to me old Nathan was a bugbear—an ogre!

Despite his angry and reiterated injunctions, she frequently brought her workbasket or book into the room where we plodded with our pens, day after day, for she loved companionship, and Nathan's churlish old housekeeper bored her.

Then sometimes, when we would be writing, and she was sewing or reading near us, I might pause, for irresistible was the temptation to turn to the soft and downcast face of Ruth; and it was strange that however deeply interested in her book—however anxious about her needlework, by some hidden or magnetic influence, she, at the same time paused, and raised her eyelids with a bright inquiring smile, that never failed to thrill my heart with joy, to make my hand tremble, and every pulse to quicken, as our glances instantly met and were instantly withdrawn.

"Here is a little bit of romance at last!" thought I; "already our thoughts and aspirations draw towards each other."

So I resolved to fall in love—most desperately in love with Ruth Wylie—and did so accordingly.

In the full bloom of girlhood, she was at an age when all girls are pretty, or may pass for being so; but Ruth was indeed charming!

She had very luxuriant hair of a colour between brown and bright auburn; its tresses were wavy rather than curly, and her complexion was of the dazzling purity which generally accompanies hair of that description, while her eyes were dark, and their lashes black as night.

Our residence in the same house brought us constantly together, and my love ripened with frightful rapidity. In three days my case was desperate, and Ruth alone could cure it. I was sleepless by night—feverish and restless by day; yet I dared scarcely to address Ruth, for love fills the heart of a boy with timidity.

On the other hand, it endues a girl with courage, and so Ruth talked to me gaily, laughed and rallied me, while my tongue faltered, my cheek flushed or grew pale, and my heart ached with love and new-born joy.

There is a strange happiness in the first love of a boy and girl—the magnetic sympathy which draws heart to heart, and lip to lip, in perfect innocence, and without a thought of the future, or of the solemn obligations of life, and of the world—the weary world, which, with all its conventionalities, is more a clog to us than we to it.

However, I soon perceived that Ruth changed colour, too, when we met; and my heart leaped joyously, when playfully she kissed her hand to me at parting. I felt that I loved her dearly and deeply, but how was I to tell her so?

In all the romances lent to me by my friend, the milliner, the tall and handsome heroes, cast their plumed beavers and ample mantles on the ground, and flung themselves on their knees before their mistresses, beseeching them, in piercing accents, to make them the happiest of men, by giving them even the tips of their snowy fingers to kiss; but I lacked the courage to imitate these striking proceedings; moreover, I possessed neither velvet mantle nor ostrich plume.

One evening, old Nathan was absent on business, and Ruth and I were seated in the recess of a window, looking at a collection of Hogarth's prints. We sat close, very close together, for the window was narrow, and then the volume was so large that we both required to hold it. I felt Ruth's breath at times upon my cheek, and our hands touched every time we turned a leaf.

Her pretty bosom, that heaved beneath her bodice, which was cut square at the neck, and somewhat low in front; her snow-white arms, that came tapering forth from the loose falling sleeves of her black dress, and her delicate little hands so bewildered me, that I never saw the prints with which we were supposed to be engrossed. I saw Ruth—Ruth only, and felt all the joy her presence inspired.

I knew that we both spoke at random, and were somewhat confused in our questions and answers; still more confused in our long pauses. I would have given the world to have clasped this plump little Ruth to my breast; yet I dared scarcely to touch her hand.

As we stooped over the print of "Love à la Mode," her bent head, her white temple, and rich soft hair touched mine, and she did not withdraw.

For a few seconds we sat thus, head reclined against head; then I panted rather than breathed, as my arm stole round her waist, and my trembling lips were pressed upon her pure forehead.

Mr. William Hogarth was permitted to fall ignominiously on the carpet; and we sat thus entwined in each other's arms for a long time—I know not how long—till the twilight deepened round us, and we were roused from our dream of happiness by a harsh and croaking voice, which exclaimed:

"Fool that I am, not to have foreseen this!"

We started and found ourselves confronted by Mr. Nathan Wylie, whose grey eyes glared in the dusk like those of a polecat, through the rims of his horn spectacles.

Poor Ruth uttered a cry and fled; but I turned boldly and faced the enemy.

"So, sir," he exclaimed, in a voice that trembled with silly rage; "so, sir, this is the way you conduct yourself in the house of a God-fearing man, who has saved you from destruction, when your whole family abandoned you! Is this your gratitude, Master Philander—this the result of those pious lessons which I have sought to instil into you? But hark you, sirrah, so sure as I stand here——"

"Mr. Wylie," I began, with all the coolness I could assume; "I beg that you——"

"Peace, you young villain, and don't attempt to bully me!" he thundered out; but, immediately adopting his usual whining tone, he added: "Peace I say, for I stand here as a rampart between you and destruction—as a watchman unto Israel. But what virtue or honour, piety or morality am I likely to find in one who bears the name of Basil Gauntlet? After what I have seen to-night, Ruth shall remain a prisoner in her own room, and I must consult with your grandfather about having you sent off to sea, or away from here on any terms."

This would have been welcome intelligence some time ago; but the presence of Ruth had altered the aspect of everything, and I retired to my attic, less to ponder over the rough manner in which we had been wakened from our dream of joy, than to repeat, react and dream it over and over again, with the sweet conviction that Ruth permitted me to love her, and loved me in return.

CHAPTER III.

THE SEQUEL.

NATHAN WYLIE was as wicked as his word; and a letter, rehearsing in forcible terms my sinful, ungracious, and godless conduct, was duly despatched to my grandfather at Netherwood Hall.

Pending a reply thereto, Ruth was confined to her own room, and kept securely under lock and key, while I was all but chained to my desk, for Nathan Wylie had an old dread of the enterprising nature of the Gauntlets, and knew not what I might do next.

In our mutual loneliness of position, our hearts naturally drew together, and our love was strengthened by the very barriers her uncle raised between us; hence I resolved to see Ruth in her own room—her prison it seemed to me; but this could only be done by the window, and under cloud of night, as her door was locked, and the key was in old Wylie's pocket.

On coming to this resolution, I proceeded at once to put it in practice. Heaven knows, I had no desire but to circumvent old Wylie, and to see my pretty Ruth—to hear her gentle voice, and to be with her, for her smile was the first ray of light that had fallen across my hitherto dark and solitary path.

It was on a gloomy night, early in February, and when the little household were supposed to be all in bed, that by slipping from the window of my attic, I reached the roof of the stable, the ridge of which I knew to be immediately under the window-sill of Ruth's apartment.

My heart beat lightly, happily, and rapidly, when I saw the shadow of Ruth's figure thrown in a somewhat colossal outline, however, upon the curtains; and, fortunately, without disturbing Abraham Clod, the groom, I reached the window, before Ruth had either retired to rest or extinguished her light.

I know that this clandestine visit was rather a wrong proceeding; but in extenuation I have only to plead the rashness of youth on one hand, and Nathan Wylie's severity on the other; besides, at eighteen one does not value the opinion of the world much, or scan such matters too closely.

On peeping in I saw Ruth pinning up her bright brown hair, and beginning to unfasten the hooks of her bodice; then her dimpled elbows and tapered arms shone white as alabaster in the light of her candle; so I hastened to tap on the window.

"Good Heaven!" she exclaimed, starting round with alarm expressed in her pretty face, and her dark eyes dilated; "what is that—who is there?"

"I, I—don't you know me?" said I, with my nose flattened against a pane of glass.

"Basil—is it Basil?"

"Yes."

"At my window, and at this time of night!" said she, blushing and hastening forward to open the sash; "wait until I get a shawl—I was just about to undress. How very odd; but what do you want?"

"To see you—to speak with you—"

"But, Basil, consider——" said she, trembling.

"I consider nothing," I exclaimed, throwing my arms round her, and kissing her at the window.

"Mercy! take care lest you fall."

"This separation renders me miserable; for two whole days I have not seen you."

Her kiss, so tender and loving, agitated me so deeply that my voice was almost inarticulate.

"And mewed up here, I have been so wretched too, dear Basil," she murmured, while placing her arms caressingly round my neck, as I crept in and closed the window; "how cruel of uncle Nathan to treat us so."

"He has written to my grandfather, and in such harsh terms that more mischief will be in store for me," said I, bitterly.

"Take courage, dear Basil," whispered Ruth, as we sat with our arms entwined and cheek pressed against flushing cheek; "those wicked people would seem to have done you already all the harm that is possible."

"I know not; for your uncle spoke of having me sent to sea; and I have heard at times of people being kidnapped by the pressgang."

"The pressgang — you!" exclaimed Ruth, her fine eyes filling with pity and indignation; "they dare not think of such a thing. Are you not the heir to a baronetcy?"

"True—one of our oldest Nova Scotian baronetcies; but so is my cousin Tony, if—if——"

"What?"

"I were sent out of the way or disposed of for ever."

"Of that title, dearest Basil, neither your grandfather's wicked hatred, nor the cunning of my uncle—alas! that I should have to say so of one so near—can deprive you."

"Between them, however, they have willed away the estates to my cousin Tony Gauntlet, who bids fair to make ducks and drakes of them, even before his succession comes to pass, for he is deeply involved with jockeys and Jew money-lenders. But I care not what happens, if I am not separated, my sweet little love, from you."

I pressed her to my breast long and passionately.

For several nights I visited Ruth's window in this clandestine manner; and became so expert in the matter, that I actually rubbed the sash of my casement with soap, that it might run smoothly and noiselessly. As yet there came no reply from Sir Basil, but Abraham Clod brought a message from Netherwood, that "he had the gout in both feet, and consequently was unable to write."

Dear to us, indeed, were those stolen interviews, and wild and vague were the plans we began to form for the future, plans chiefly drawn from our romances; but one night we were roused from our happiness by an unlooked for catastrophe.

Just as I was approaching Ruth's window, a voice exclaimed—

"A thief—a thief! I see un—dang thee, tak that!"

Then followed a shriek from Ruth, with the explosion of a gun, and a bullet shattered the panes in both sashes, just above my head.

It was the voice of Abraham Clod our Yorkshire groom, who had been out in the evening crowshooting, and had his gun undischarged, and who in a moment of evil had seen me creeping along the roof of the stable, from his attic window, where I saw him peering forth, with a candle in one hand, and his gun in the other.

Fearing that if I attempted to return to my own room he might shoot me in earnest —for I saw the fellow was quickly reloading—fearing also to stay, lest I should place Ruth in a false position, I lingered for a moment irresolutely, and preferred being taken for the housebreaker which I have no doubt honest Clod believed me to be.

At that time I felt that I would rather die than the honour of Ruth should suffer!

I dropped on the roof of the stable just as a second shot broke the tiles under my feet, and confused by this incident, I tumbled heavily to the ground—luckily not into the stable-yard but into a ploughed field.

I rose unhurt, but found that to enter

the house by the door, and to regain my attic window, were both impossible now. I struck across the fields, gained the high-road, and took my way into the open country with sorrow and rage in my heart —sorrow for Ruth, and rage at her uncle, whose drudge and fool I resolved no longer to be.

CHAPTER IV.

MY COUSIN TONY.

"UNDER the roof of his home," says a pleasing writer, "the boy feels *safe;* and where in the whole realm of life, with its bitter toils and its bitterer temptations, will he ever feel *safe* again?"

I had no roof-tree—I had never felt this charming safety or security—this sublime knowledge of home, and keenly came this conviction to my heart, as I walked on that dark February night along the solitary highway, with the rain plashing in my face; for now, as if to add to the misery of my situation, the clouds had gathered in heaven and the rain fell heavily.

An old fir-tree with its thick dark foliage sheltered me for a time. Towards daybreak the weather became fair, and after sleeping for some hours in a hayrick, I set forward again. I knew that I must present but a sorry figure, but cared not. I was always a lover of effect, and hoped it might aid me in my purpose, which was to urge Sir Basil to make some fitting provision for me.

Alas! I was ignorant that he had actually written to Nathan Wylie, desiring that the pittance allowed me should be withdrawn, and that he was to turn me adrift for ever. The old minister of Netherwood, who was with him when this severe answer was despatched, besought him to "be clement, and to remember that he too had once been young."

"Yes," growled the gruff baronet, "but it is so very long ago that I have forgotten all about it. Zounds!" he added, flourishing his crutch, and smashing a wine decanter, "I'll make that young dog smart for this, as I made his father smart before him!"

His orders Mr. Nathan Wylie would cheerfully have obeyed; but in the end I may show how the lawyer, even in the matter of the will, *outwitted himself*, as he might, but for his hatred of my father's memory, and his slavish obsequiousness to Sir Basil, have made little Ruth one day Lady of Netherwood, and me, perhaps, his friend for ever.

On that dull February eve I knew nothing of all this, and so trod on for several miles with hope in my breast—hope that I might stir some chord of sympathy in the withered heart of Sir Basil; but when I drew near Netherwood, and saw its copper vanes and antique turrets shining above the trees, my spirit failed me, and I thought with just indignation of my favoured cousin Tony, of his probable mockery at the sorry figure I presented, and the quiet insolence of the domestics; so I sat by the wayside inspired only by that bitterness and irresolution which I have described in the opening of my story.

To Nathan Wylie's house I would never return.

I sorrowed for poor Ruth, the sweet companion of so many stolen interviews—the secret love of my boyish heart. But to what end was this sorrow? Marriage and the responsibilities of life had never occurred to me. I felt, like a boy, that I loved Ruth dearly, and that was all.

I would go away somewhere—where, it mattered not; I would seek a path for myself; another time—a year hence, perhaps—I would come back and see Ruth again, if Fortune smiled on me. And with such thoughts as these, my sadness and dejection gave place to the springy and joyous conviction of a young heart—that I was free—absolutely FREE—the master of my own person—the arbiter of my own destiny!

The wide world was all before me, and to leave care and trouble behind should be now my task and duty.

How was this to be achieved? I was the possessor only of a shilling; but greater men than I have begun the world with less.

As these ideas occurred to me, I perceived in the twilight a gentleman with two valets in livery, all well mounted, coming along the road with their nags at a trot. He wore a green sporting suit, with large gilt buttons, yellow buckskin breeches, a jockey cap, and carried a heavy hunting-whip.

As the two valets were not riding behind, but were abreast with their master, and conversing with him in loud and noisy familiarity, I soon recognised my cousin Tony the Foxhunter, an interview with whom I would fain have avoided; but he knew me at once, and came brusquely up, checking his horse, with foam upon its bit, so close to me, that I was nearly knocked over.

"Zounds, cousin Basil!" said he, insolently, and in the hearing of his valets, "you are in a fine scrape now!"

"How, sir?" said I, sourly.

"So you have levanted from old Wylie's —or been turned adrift—'tis all one, for making love to his niece—eh—is this true?"

"I have no confidences to make to you,

sir," said I, haughtily, for the idea that I had placed Ruth—she so innocent and pure—in a position so false, filled me with remorse and rage.

"No confidences," stammered Tony; "eh—damme?"

"None."

"Oh, it is of no use denying it; we have just ridden from old Wylie's this morning. We don't blame you for making love to the girl—she is deuced pretty, and we all agreed it was just what we should have done ourselves."

"*We*—who do you speak of?"

"Why, Tom, Dick, and myself," he replied, pointing to his servants; "and no bad judges either of the points and paces of a woman or a horse."

"Rein back from the footpath if you please, Mr. Gauntlet, and permit me to pass," I added, for he had me completely hemmed against a hedge.

"Well, but what are you going to do *now*, for we can have no onhangers idling about Netherwood Hall?" he exclaimed, imperiously.

Instead of replying, I took his horse by the bridle, thrust its head aside, and passed disdainfully on, for I saw that he had been dining, and was flushed alike with wine and insolence. Anthony was four years older than I, and had seen much more of the world; yet, so far as education or accomplishments were concerned, this pet of my grandfather was nearly as ignorant as the grooms and stable-boys who were his constant companions and chosen friends, and who, in those capacities, fleeced him of large sums on the turf, in the tavern, and at the gaming-table.

"Did you hear me speak, fellow?" he thundered out, with an oath, while urging his horse close behind me, as if to ride me down.

Instead of turning, I quickened my pace; but he and his grooms put spur to their nags and followed me.

"S'blood!" exclaimed Tony, "but this will make you *feel* if you cannot hear me!" and he dealt me a heavy lash across the shoulders with his hunting-whip.

With all the strength and fury that a long sense of unmerited wrong, hardship, neglect, and opprobrium could inspire, I rushed upon this usurper of my patrimony, and in a moment he was torn from his saddle and stretched upon the highway. I wrenched away his whip, and, twisting the lash round my wrist, beat him soundly with the handle.

Being stronger than I, he scrambled up,

with his green coat covered with dust and his features inflamed by rage; he closed with me, swearing frightfully, while his two mounted followers assailed me in the rear with their clubbed whips.

"Lay on, Dick! lay on, Tom!" he cried repeatedly; "d—n him, beat the beggarly rascal's brains out!"

I received several severe blows on the head and shoulders, while Tony actually strove to strangle me by twisting my neck-tie; and in a combat so unequal I must have been defeated and severely handled in the end, had not two men who were clad in long scarlet cloaks, and were mounted on grey horses, interposed, and one who had drawn his sword, exclaimed—

"Hold, fellows, hold! What the devil do you mean—is it murder? Back! on your lives, stand back! Why this cowardly attack of three upon one?"

On this the valets precipitately withdrew a little way; but Tony still grasped my collar, and on perceiving by their dress and accoutrements that the interposers were two Horse Grenadiers or Dragoons, he swore at them roundly, and said—

"What value do you put upon your ears that you dare to accost me upon the highway?"

"Dare?" repeated the soldier, contemptuously.

"Yes, dare!" exclaimed my cousin, foaming with rage. "Be off with you. Do you imagine that a scurvy trooper can scare me? I am Anthony Gauntlet of Netherwood Hall, and in the commission of the peace for this county; so begone I say, or d—n me I'll put you both in the stocks at the nearest market cross."

The dragoon laughed, and placed the

bare blade of his sword so close to Tony's neck that he hastily released me and slunk back.

"If you are what you say, sir," observed the other dragoon, with a singular hauteur in his tone and manner, "a justice of the peace, you should not be brawling thus with people on the king's highway."

"Rascal, to whom do you presume to give advice, eh?" roared Tony, choking with passion.

"Double rascal, to you!" thundered out the soldier, as he wrenched away by a single twitch of his right hand one of the valets' whips, and lashed Tony and his fellows so soundly, and with such rapidity, that they scarcely knew whether they were on the highway or in the air.

He fairly drove them off, while his comrade, who had now sheathed his sword, sat in his saddle and laughed heartily as he looked on.

"Come with us, my lad," said he, "lest those cowardly curs return and fall on you again. There is an inn somewhere near this, I believe—or at least there was when last we marched into England."

"Yes, you mean the 'Marquis of Granby,'" said I, while applying my handkerchief to a cut on my left temple, which bled profusely.

"Ah! that is the place I mean; we must find our quarters there for the night. You will share a glass with us and tell us how this battle came to pass?"

And to this invitation I assented.

CHAPTER V.

THE INN.

MY protectors proved to be two of the Second Dragoons, or Scots Greys—a corporal and a private—who had been escorting a couple of prisoners, captured smugglers, to the Tolbooth of Dunbar, and who were proceeding to rejoin their regiment, which was then quartered at the nearest market town on the English side of the Border.

"Kirkton, what did that fellow with the jockey cap call himself?" asked the corporal.

"I scarcely heard; but he said he was a justice of the peace."

"A rare one, certainly! But he cannot meddle with us, Tom, for we are on duty until we rejoin. Why did he attack you, my lad?" asked the corporal, turning to me; "were you poaching?"

"No," said I, angrily, though the state of my attire perfectly warranted the inference; "but here is the inn."

It was a common wayside hostelry, where the Berwick stages changed horses in those days—a two-storied house, with a large stable-yard behind and an ivy-clad porch in front; over the latter hung a square signboard that creaked in the wind on an iron rod, and bore a profile of the Marquis of Granby in a bright red coat and white brigadier wig, with the information beneath, that within was "good entertainment for man and beast."

The landlord knit his brows and muttered something surly, under his breath however, on seeing the two dragoons approach; but Jack Charters, the corporal, presented a slip of printed paper, saying—

"How are you, old boy? Here is our billet order."

"From whom?" growled Boniface.

"The billet master. . To-morrow it will be from a constable, but then we shall be in England."

Perceiving that the host scowled at the document—

"It is quite correct, my dear friend," began the corporal, in a bantering tone, "and quite in the terms of the Billeting Act, which extends to all inns, livery stables, and houses of persons selling brandy, strong waters, cider and metheglin, whatever the devil that may be."

And then, laughing merrily, they rode straight into the stable-yard, where they unsaddled, stalled and groomed their horses with soldierlike rapidity, and taking care to stand by while each had its feed of corn, for they knew too much of the world to trust to an ostler's nice sense of honour.

Then we repaired to the bar of the inn, where the entrance of a couple of dashing dragoons in braided uniforms and high bearskin caps, with all their accoutrements rattling about them, created somewhat of a sensation.

The rosy-cheeked barmaid smiled with pleasure, the plump landlady curtsied twice, even the ungracious host pushed forward a couple of chairs—I was permitted to find one for myself—and several bumpkins took their long clay pipes from their mouths, and gazed with admiration, for the appearance of two scarlet coats in this peaceful quarter of

Great Britain was quite an epoch in its history.

"Bustle, landlady, if you please," said the corporal, "and get us something to eat by way of supper."

"Supper for three," added the private, with a quick glance at me; "nay, no refusal, my lad," he added, interrupting some apology I was about to make, with an empty purse, an aching heart, and a burning cheek; "many a time I have known the pleasure of supping, yea, and dining too, at a friend's expense."

These dragoons were men who had an air, bearing, and tone far above their subordinate rank in the service, and there was a mystery about this that could not fail to interest me.

They were both bold and handsome fellows, with eyes that looked steadily at men, and saucily at women; slashing troopers, with long strides, huge spurs, and steel scabbards that made a terrible jingling.

The corporal pinched the landlady's chin, and then gave the landlord a slap on the back which nearly made him swallow a foot-length of his clay pipe, as they seated themselves.

"For shame!" said the barmaid, as our enterprising non-commissioned officer slipped an arm round her waist; "I fear you are a very bad fellow."

"I would rather be that than a *sad* fellow," said he; "but get us supper quick, my pretty one; we have had a long ride on a cold February day; but pray don't make a fuss, my dear—for me at least; I have long been used to take the world as it comes."

The landlord, who had not yet digested his mouthful of pipe, grumbled, as if to say that "private soldiers were not the kind of guests they were used to make a fuss about;" but he dared not speak aloud, for the aspect of his two unexpected visitors rather awed him, and the female portion of the household were all in their favour.

A piece of roasted beef, cold, some bread, and the materials for manufacturing whisky toddy, were rapidly laid for us within a snug recess that opened off the bar. A large fire which blazed within the wide arched fireplace, filled the whole apartment with a ruddy light, that was reflected from scores of plates in a rack, and rows of polished tin and pewter mugs and tankards; but I selected a seat that was in shadow, for Farmer Flail, who was seated in an arm-chair close by, and had wakened up at the noise of our entrance, had dozed off to sleep, and I had no wish to be recognised if he awoke again.

Although I was scarcely a mile from the avenue of Netherwood, old Roger Flail was the only person in that district who knew me.

"The last time I was in this quarter, a strange affair happened," said the corporal.

"How?" I inquired.

"Our chaplain fought a duel."

"A duel—your chaplain?"

"Yes—with a cornet of Bland's Horse."

"About some point of scripture?"

"About a pretty girl, and the poor cornet was run through the body, and left dead, near the gate of a hall—Netherwood, I think 'tis called."

"Were you in the Greys, then?" I inquired.

"No—I was in the Dragoon Guards, and I had *not* the honour to be a corporal," he replied, while a dark expression stole over his handsome and sunburnt face.

"Have you seen service?" I asked.

The troopers laughed.

"Seen service!" repeated the corporal; "I have seen everything—the devil himself, I believe; but we have both smelt powder in Flanders, and hope to do so soon again. Another slice of the beef, my boy? No more, you say? At your age, I could have eaten a horse behind the saddle."

I begged to be excused; I had but little appetite.

"I hope you can drink, at all events," said Tom Kirkton, the private, pushing the jug of hot water and the whisky bottle towards me; "make your brewage and be jolly while you may."

Then while stirring his steaming

punch, in a full, deep, manly voice, he began to sing, while the corporal clanked his spurs and clinked his glass in tune to the favourite camp song of the day.

"How stands the glass around?
For shame, ye take no care, my boys!
How stands the glass around?
Let mirth and wine abound!
The trumpets sound,
And the colours flying are, my boys,
To fight, kill, or wound;
May we still be found,
Content with our hard fare, my boys,
On the cold ground!

"Why, soldiers, why
Should we be melancholy, boys?
Why, soldiers, why,
Whose business 'tis to die?
What, sighing?—fie!
Shun fear, drink on, be jolly, boys!
'Tis he, you, or I,
Cold, hot, wet, or dry,
We're always bound to follow, boys,
And scorn to fly.

"'Tis but in vain
(I mean not to upbraid you, boys)
'Tis but in vain
For soldiers to complain ;
Should next campaign,
Send us to HIM who made us, boys,
We're free from pain ;
But should we remain,
A bottle and kind landlady
Cures all again."

As he concluded, Kirkton kissed the hostess, and ordered another bottle.

"When I was in the Dragoon Guards, at the siege of Maestricht," said the corporal, with something sad in his tone, "six of us sang that song one night in my tent; before the noon of next day, there was but one alive of all the six—myself—who could better have been spared."

"You look downcast, my lad," said Kirkton to me.

"Ay," added the corporal; "what is the matter? have you done aught that is likely to make you seek a healthier atmosphere?"

"Don't jibe the poor fellow, Jack," said the other on perceiving a flush of annoyance cross my face.

"Is love at the bottom of it?"

"See how he reddens—of course it is."

"You mistake," said I, with a bitter sigh; "my funds are at *zero*."

"Is that all?" observed the corporal, laughing; "mine have been so many times, for Fortune is a fickle wench; but, egad! the dice-box, a little prize money, a present from a pretty woman, or something else, always made the silver rise again to blood heat. Well—and so your purse is empty?"

"As you see—there is but a shilling in it."

"When mine was thus, I took another in the king's name, and then I had *two*—

by that stroke I exactly doubled my fortune. What is your profession?"

"I have none."

"Relations?"

"Yes," I replied, flushing to the temples with anger.

"Friends, I should have said."

"None."

"Right!" exclaimed Corporal Charters, bitterly; "friends and relations are often very different people."

"Come," added Kirkton, "be one of us—you are just a lad after old Preston's heart."

"Old Preston—who is he?"

"Zounds, man! don't you know? He is Colonel of the Greys—our idol! we all love the old boy as if he was our father—and a father he is indeed to the whole regiment. Come, then, I say, be one of us—the lads who are second to none."

"*Second to none!*" echoed the corporal, draining his glass with enthusiasm, for this is yet the proud motto of his regiment; "you have still your brave heart, boy—the king will give you a sword, and you will ride with us against the French as a Scots Grey dragoon."

The fumes of the potent alcohol I was imbibing had already mounted to my head; the idea of becoming a soldier had freouentiy occurred to me, and these roopers had only anticipated a proposal I was about to make them.

"I will—I will!" I exclaimed, and gave each my hand upon the promise. Another jorum of punch was ordered, and long before it was finished, I found myself wearing the corporal's grenadier cap and aiguilettes, girded with his comrade's sword and belt, seated on the table, and singing most lustily, I know not what.

Then I thought of Ruth, and becoming sad related to them my love affair, at which they shocked me very much by laughing loudly, and for their own amusement made me describe her hair, eyes, hands and voice again and again, as I had drunk too deeply to perceive how they quizzed me. However after a time, it seemed to me, that they too became maudlin, as they rehearsed several of their tender experiences.

"There was a time," said the Corporal, "when I too imagined I could love a girl for ever."

"For ever is a long time, Jack!"

"I still love with ardour—"

"For a day," suggested Kirkton, and then he added, with a tipsy air of sentimental sadness, "love sheds a halo over everything, and brings us nearer heaven."

"Indeed! By Jove, it nearly sent me

the *other* way once, and almost brought me to a General Court Martial."

"Oh—you mean your scrape with—"

"The countess—yes—but silence on that matter, Tom," replied the corporal, whose face flushed, and he gave a bitter smile.

There was a pause during which, though very tipsy, I surveyed him with interest, for every line of his face expressed stern loftiness, and then something of sadness and mortification.

"Well—well," said Kirkton, "drink and forget."

"No—no more for me, and you, Tom, have had quite enough."

"Bah! another glass—for sobriety, there is not my equal in the service—in the Greys most certainly—"

"How stands the glass around?
For shame, ye take no care, my boys!"

Of this night I remember no more, than falling asleep—I am ashamed to say—across the table, during Kirkton's song, completely overcome by what I had imbibed; and thus ended the first episode of my new career.

CHAPTER VI.

ENLISTMENT.

EARLY morning brought sobriety, with a headache, a burning thirst, and deep reflection.

I had enlisted as a private dragoon: I, the heir to a baronetcy; but it was a baronetcy that would not bring with it an acre of land, and by the enmity of its present possessors, I was then on the verge of total want. What other path was open to me than this, which it seemed as if the hand of destiny now indicated?

"Yes—yes," thought I, "it is the *dictum* of fate!"

My position had been one of extreme difficulty. I could not dig, and to beg

—even from Sir Basil—I was ashamed besides, I had a spirit that revolted at the idea of eating bread that was won eitner by falsehood or servility.

" 'Tis done!" said I, thinking aloud, " in the plain red coat of a trooper, none will ever discover Basil Gauntlet--the disinherited heir of Netherwood!"

" So you are still resolved to be one o us?" said Charters, when we met early in the morning.

" Yes."

" 'Tis well; life is a lottery—let us go and draw," he observed, figuratively.

" I would rather go and drink," added Kirkton, who, after our late potations, looked rather red about the eyes.

" Try a dram—and then hey for the road; but we must have our new comrade attested. Landlord, where is a justice of the peace to be found?"

"Plague on them—they're thick as blackberries on both sides o' the Border," growled the host.

"For one, there is Nathan Wylie, the writer at—" began the hostess.

"No—no—I go not before *him!*" said I, with a pang of sorrow in my heart, as I thought of Ruth, whose sweet image came upbraidingly to my memory.

"Well—who next?" asked the corporal, while buckling on his sword.

"Sir Basil Gauntlet, at the hall—or his nephew, the young Laird that is to be."

"Worse still!" I exclaimed, passionately; "I shall not go before them either."

"Zounds, but you are hard to please," said Charters as he eyed me keenly, but with something of commiseration too. "What is your name?"

"That I shall tell the magistrate," I replied, evasively, not having yet thought of a *nom de guerre*. Then the corporal asked me—

"Is this Sir Basil a relation, a connection, or what?"

The landlord laughed while eyeing my scurvy appearance, as if he thought it very unlikely I could be either; my breast burned with suppressed mortification and rage, but I continued calmly,

"It matters little—I go not before him."

"You are regularly enlisted, my lad," said the corporal, soothingly, "and must go before some one."

"Try the rector," said I.

"We have no rectors in Scotland," said the landlord, bluntly.

"Well, there is one over the Border, a few miles from this——"

"On the road to Rothbury—good," said Charters.

"He is a justice of the peace, and such a one! Odsbud! he sent a child, four years old, to hard labour for having a tame pheasant for a pet."

"How?"

"As a poacher," added Boniface, with a rough malediction.

"Will *he* do?" asked the Corporal.

"Yes," said I, briefly; "and now let us begone."

"Bravo! Now, Kirkton—brandy and water—boot and saddle, and let us be off. Our new comrade shall share our horses alternately, for we have nearly twenty miles to travel to-day before we reach head-quarters."

As the troopers brought from the stable to the inn door their two stately grey chargers, in all the trappings of a heavy dragoon regiment, with saddle-cloth, scarlet valise, long holsters, powerful bits, and chain bridles, an old horse that was passing, heavily laden with the wares of an itinerant basket-maker, pricked up his ears, and switched his short shorn tail, and seemed to eye us wistfully.

"That is an old trooper," said Kirkton; "by Jove, the poor animal actually recognises our red coats, and, doubtless, his heart warms to the colour. Landlord, a feed of oats, and here is the money for it—a feed of oats for the old nag-tailed trooper. He has been a heavy dragoon horse—see here are the white spots where the carbine has galled him. Well, well! it makes one sad to think that the dashing horse, which has perhaps borne a brave fellow in many a charge, which has fed from his hand, and slept beside him in the bivouac, comes down to the sand cart and knacker's yard at last!"

"After all, his rider's fate is seldom

better in the end," said the corporal, "and I don't think either you or I, Tom, will have our tombs in Westminster Abbey. But bring the brandy; confound care and reflection; let us live while we can and be jolly, too!"

I rode each of their horses alternately after we crossed the Border, as we proceeded southward, along the road towards the Rectory.

My comrades were rather silent now, and I was often left to my own reflections. The day was gloomy and lowering, and the wind came in gusts; dark clouds rolled in masses across the grey, sullen sky; the distant Cheviot hills looked brown and sombre; but nature's aspect failed to impress me with gloom as on the preceding day.

I felt a glow of new enthusiasm kindling in my heart. The hopes inspired by ambition, pride, and all a boy's visions of military pomp and glory, grew strong within me. To wear a fine uniform—to ride a showy horse—to be a captain in a year—to return to the village—to marry Ruth—and to flaunt my finery before the people, were my most prominent ideas. A year? Amid all this, I remembered that my dashing comrade, Jack Charters, spoke of having been a soldier for *ten* years, and was only a corporal still!

This was far from encouraging; but then I should be certain to prove so much more sober, steady, and industrious than Jack; and so I rode on scheming out my future career, with great brilliance and rapidity, and much to my own satisfaction.

I was full of such thoughts when we reached the gate of the Rectory, which was a quaint old building, having its deeply embayed and mullioned windows nearly hidden by luxuriant masses of ivy, vine and clematis. It was small, and covered simply with bright yellow thatch; but its walls were thick and strong, though they had often been subjected to fire by the invading Scots, in the stormy times of old.

We left the horses at the gothic porch, and, by a servant in livery, were ushered into the library, where the Rector was seated at luncheon, with a decanter of port before him, and he had been evidently dozing over his books and papers.

To attest recruits at once, without the many formalities of medical inspections and so forth, was common in those days, and for long after. Had it been otherwise, the public would never have been favoured with the memoirs of Phœbe Hassel, who served seven years in

H. M. 5th Foot, or of Mrs. Christian Davis, another woman, who served in all the battles of Marlborough, as a trooper in the Scots Greys, who had her head fractured by the splinter of a shell at Ramilies, and who enjoyed a pension of one shilling per diem till she died, and was buried with military honours in the ground belonging to Chelsea Hospital.*

The Rector was a fine old gentleman, with a mild and rubicund visage; and he had been, I knew, my father's early friend and schoolfellow; so I resolved to enter the service under some such name as Smith or Brown instead of my own.

He started from his waking dream as the two dragoons clattered in. I can still see, in memory, that quaint old library in

* "Records of the Scots Greys," pp. 49-51. Phœbe Hassel was alive at Brighton in 1821. She served in the West Indies, and at Gibraltar.

which he received us, with its dark oak shelves of goodly folios and quartos, in calf bindings, dark and brown; some partial gleams of sunlight streaming through the lozenged window panes and carved stone mullions fell on the old man's shining head and scattered silver hairs—on the floor of polished oak, on the furniture of walnut wood, and on the russet tints that time had cast over everything.

"What bring you here, my friends—not a deserter—this boy?" stammered the Rector, with sadness and pity in his eye and tone, while wheeling his elbow chair half round.

"No, no, reverend sir, a recruit," replied Charters, with a military salute; "a recruit whom we wish you to attest."

"That slender boy for the cavalry!" exclaimed the Rector.

"He will do excellently for the troop

of light horse which Captain Lindsay of ours is raising," suggested Kirkton.

I was then slightly formed, and looked, I knew, wan, dejected, and poor. The good rector surveyed me through his gold-rimmed spectacles with an unmistakeable expression of pity on his benign and fatherly face; after a pause—

"Have you considered this matter well?" he asked; "but you look weary, my poor lad! take some wine—there are glasses on the buffet—corporal, help yourself."

"I thank your Reverence," said Charters, who never required a second invitation of this kind, and so filled our glasses with port—his own twice in succession, and drank, muttering, "Good stuff this! I've tasted worse—in a palace too."

"Have you weighed well the step you

are about to take?" continued the rector, impressively.

"Yes," said I, firmly.

"But your parents——" he urged gently: "think of them."

"I have none," said I, in tones that faltered as my heart swelled with emotion, and the old man shook his head sadly.

"You will never be able to undergo the hardships of foreign service," said he, shaking his head.

"Then I will help to fill the trenches," said I, with that spirit of bravado which we so often feel or assume in youth.

The corporal said something approvingly; then the rector sighed, as he dipped a pen in an inkhorn, and placed on his desk a printed document, preparatory to filling up the blanks, or fifteen replies to questions always asked of a recruit at attestation.

"What is your name?" he began.

Now it was that my heart failed me, and the question had to be repeated three times, as I could not tell an untruth.

"Do you hear me," he added, gently; "your name?"

"Basil Gauntlet."

He threw down the pen and half rose from his chair.

"The son of Major Gauntlet, of Granby's Dragoons?"

"Yes," I replied, while both of the soldiers turned, and faced me inquiringly, and with unconcealed interest in their eyes.

"Oh, Basil," exclaimed the rector, who knew at once both me and my story, "this is sad, most sad. Consider, I pray you, consider well. I have some right to say this, for your father was one of my dearest and earliest friends."

"Sir, you know how *his* father has treated me; thus, that which might have been dire necessity at first, has now become my choice. I am resolved to be a soldier, so I beg of you to hasten over this most mortifying scene, and let me begone."

In the irritation I felt at my position, I spoke somewhat sternly, even ungraciously, to this good man; so Charters came to my aid, and urged that time pressed, so the formal oath was administered, which bound me "faithfully and honestly to defend his Majesty King George, his heirs and successors, in person, crown, and dignity, against all enemies, and to obey all the orders of his Majesty, his heirs and successors, and of the generals and officers set over me," &c.

This oath made me irrevocably a soldier.

The old rector shook my hand, and his voice faltered, for he felt more emotion than I did, as he accompanied us to the porch of his house, where he kindly bade us adieu.

"We shall have a most disastrous war ere long," said he, "and I may say in the words of Goldsmith, 'Go, my boy, and if you fall, though distant, exposed and unwept for a time, by those who love you, the most precious tears are those with which Heaven bedews the unburied head of the soldier.' Farewell, my friends. God bless you!"

"We thank you, sir," replied Charters, with a profound salute, and with an air that had something lofty and noble in it, as he sprang on his horse and gathered up his reins; "a good man's blessing can never be given in vain, especially to such reckless dogs as we are; but, believe me, sir, that though but poor soldiers now, my comrades and I can never forget that we have been, and may again be, *gentlemen!*"

We were once more on the open highway. I was glad the scene was over, but I still seemed to see the mild and benevolent face of the old rector, and to hear his parting words.

"So we have really had the honour of enlisting the heir to a baronetcy?" said Kirkton. "You were right to come with us. I thought you were meant for better things than to be squire to a knight of the bluebag."

"What is that?"

"A lawyer. Were we quartered in Bath your story would make your fortune. Any heiress would marry you for the prospect of the title."

"That is flattering," said I; and then

thinking of Ruth, I added, "Why not for love?"

"Bah!" said Charters, "people don't marry for that, except in plays and novels."

"Jack, you are a misanthrope in spite of yourself," said Kirkton; "but as this youth is the heir to a baronetcy——"

"I beg to have your promises of keeping the matter a secret when we reach the regiment?" said I, with great earnestness.

"Why?" asked they.

"Because I owe nothing to my family, and hate them as they hate me—the living at least. Whatever I may do to gain honour or promotion, will never be acknowledged by my comrades, who will be certain to attribute success to the fortuitous circumstance of family and name."

"Egad! you are right, boy, and I love and respect your spirit," said Charters. "I have more than once seen a poor fellow gain the ill-will and malevolence of his comrades for being better born or better bred than those among whom his lot was cast, and thus bitterness came with prosperity."

"Your solemn pledge, then, that you will keep my secret?" said I, earnestly.

They promised, and I may add that the worthy fellows never betrayed it; but they too had each a secret, which they confided to me as we sat together over a glass of beer in a wayside tavern, a few miles from Rothbury.

"If I had not had the misfortune to have been born a genius, I should perhaps never have been a soldier," said Kirkton.

"A genius—you?" exclaimed the corporal, laughing.

"Sorry am I to say it, for 'tis the fate of geniuses to be restless and unfortunate. True; Boetus, who wrote on the battle of Philippi, died in prison; Plautus was a baker's drudge and turned a hand-mill; Terentius Publius was the slave of a Roman senator——. And I, Thomas Kirkton, am a private in the Scots Greys!"

"'Tis an ungrateful world, my friends," added the other, with an air of tragi-comedy that made us both laugh.

CHAPTER VII.

MY COMRADES.

Tom Kirkton was the son of a thrifty and prudent Scottish clergyman, who had educated him for the Church, in the hope that he might be his assistant and successor; but the wild life led by Tom when at college, a natural impetuosity of temper, a genius for everything but application—rash adventures and excitements—with stories of nights spent in gambling and carousing, and rumours of various *intrigues d'amour*, led to his formal expulsion by the Reverend Principal, and ultimately drove him into the ranks of the Scots Greys.

Time and experience had somewhat

tempered the reckless tenor of his ways, and, though his boisterous manner was rather startling at times, I could not but deem myself fortunate in having a companion so well educated as he.

The story of Charters was indeed a singular one.

Five miles north-east of Dumfries there stands a tall, square, and ancient fortress called the Castle of Amisfield, between the two head streams of the Lochar. For centuries this great tower had been the stronghold and residence of the Scoto-Norman family of Charters, of whom my comrade, the corporal, was the last representative.

In that tower he was born and reared, until he joined the army as an officer. At the age of eighteen he found himself a lieutenant in the 1st Dragoon Guards, and the inheritor of a splendid fortune, which he lavished in London with the reckless prodigality of a Timon. He was at that time on leave of absence, seeking a transfer into a light dragoon regiment.

When rambling one night near Hyde-park Corner, he heard the cries of a lady whose carriage had been stopped by foot-pads. He hurried to her rescue, and narrowly escaped a pistol-shot; but, closing with the fellow who fired it, struck him down, on which his companions fled, leaving Charters in possession of the field of battle.

The rescued lady proved to be a foreigner of very attractive face and figure, with bright blue eyes, and a profusion of fair hair, amid which, as well as on her neck and arms, many diamonds were sparkling. She was richly dressed, and was returning, apparently, from a ball.

"You will permit me, madam, to escort

you home?" said Charters, bowing, hat in hand.

She entreated that he would not give himself so much trouble.

"But, madam," urged Charters, "those fellows may return, and I cannot rest until I know that you are safe in your own residence."

"But which is your way, sir?"

"Your way is mine, madam—nay, I insist upon it." And with great gallantry he sprang up beside the servant on the footboard behind the carriage, and the lady, pleased, perhaps, to see that he was a handsome young man, made no further objection to his escort.

"Drive home," said she.

Pleased with the adventure, and considerably attracted by the personal charms of the lady, especially by her broken English, which had a child-like lisp in its sound, Charters slipped a handsome *douceur* into the hand of the footman as the carriage rumbled along, and asked the name of his lady; but the man proved to be a foreigner also, and replied in German, of which the questioner knew not a word.

"Good!" said Charters; "the mystery increases."

Indeed it grew greater still when the carriage, after traversing the Park by the bank of the Serpentine, drew up before the lighted portal of a large and handsome edifice of brick, having no less than three spacious quadrangles, ornamented with columns, quoins, and elaborate cornices of stone. Charters immediately recognised Kensington Palace. Save the porch—near which stood two sentinels of the Foot Guards in their boxes—and one or two windows, the whole façade of the building was enveloped in darkness, for the king was absent, having gone on what proved to be his last visit to Hanover.

Charters assisted the fair unknown to alight, and led her to the door of the palace, with an air of confidence so perfect, that anyone might have supposed the house to be his own. Then she perceived that he wore the Windsor uniform, at that time the usual dress of all officers when on leave or on half-pay. Attracted, no doubt, by his air, which, though gentle and soft to her, was proud, dashing, and careless, she paused upon the threshold to thank him for his ready courage and escort —then, after a little pretty hesitation, added, that she could not think of permitting him to retire without joining her at supper.

"I cannot but accept, madam," said he, kissing her right hand, from which she had coquettishly drawn the kid glove, as if, perhaps, to show its beauty.

"You have no fear?" she whispered, with a soft side-glance in her clear blue eye, as she took his proffered arm.

"None, madam; moreover, I am the foe of all restraint and prejudice."

"Then you should not have become a soldier."

"I can understand the restraints of the service, but I cannot abide the shallow and hackneyed usages of society."

It seemed to Charters that her little hand pressed his arm rather palpably at that moment, and she whispered—

"If seen here—if known—"

"By whom?" asked Charters, hastily. "You have no husband, I hope?"

"No—nor lover--none here at least," replied the lady, laughing, as she threw off her white silk capuchin or hood, and then Charters saw quite enough of fair ringlets, and a neck and shoulders of great beauty and wondrous delicacy, to remove any scruples or fears which had occurred to him. He was in for an adventure now, and felt himself compelled to go through with it. A retreat was not to be thought of.

"By what name am I to have the honour of addressing you?" asked Charters, in a half-whisper, as they sat down to supper, with the German valet in close attendance, and in a snug little room in that portion of the palace which had been built by the Lord Chancellor Finch. It was panelled and richly gilded, and from the walls one or two dark Holbeins looked grimly down upon their *tête-à-tête*. "Pray tell me, madam," he urged; "for I am dying of curiosity."

"Call me Sophia," said the lady, looking

down for a moment, and then bending her bright eyes on him smilingly; "and you?" she inquired.

"I am Lieutenant Charters, of the 1st Dragoon Guards," replied the other. "Sophia?" he repeated, in a soft, low voice, as he mentally ran over all the names of the female members of the royal family, for he concluded that his new friend must be a princess at least. Thus some very wild ideas began to float through his busy brain; but at that moment he could remember no Sophia among all the ladies who were about the Court.

Amid all the rings that glittered on her hand—and a beautiful little hand it was—he could see no plain marriage hoop; so his mind felt considerably relieved on that score. The valet in attendance wore the royal livery; but an earl's coronet and the letter Y were on all the plate, and graven somewhat ostentatiously, too.

Though some years his senior, this lady, by the charm of her manner, her wit, and conversation, bewildered Charters so much, that in less than an hour he was desperately in love with her; but she seemed resolved to preserve her incognita, and they separated, with an arrangement, however, to meet next day in Hyde Park, at an early hour, and before it was thronged by promenaders.

In short, they met frequently there, and oftener still in the green alleys of old Kensington Gardens—I mean that portion of them which was laid out by Wise, the gardener of Queen Anne; and Charters' love for his unknown became a confirmed passion, so much so that he thought of visiting the Horse Guards and withdrawing his application for a transfer to a light dragoon regiment, as he now anticipated with dread a separation from his captivating Sophia.

As she expressed a wish to visit the opera one night, he begged permission to escort her there; and on their entrance all eyes were turned towards them. Her fine hair was dressed to perfection; her bright eyes sparkled; her soft cheek was flushed with pleasure, and the richness of her dress and the splendour of her diamonds so enhanced her fair and remarkable beauty, that Charters was enchanted and felt proud of her.

Yet he could not conceal from himself that she was the object of more than common — and more than well-bred — interest. The ladies whispered to each other behind their fans, and some of the gentlemen looked at Sophia so boldly and so laughingly, that Charters felt inclined to teach them a rough lesson, if he could but fix upon one or two in particular.

They had seats next the royal box, which was empty, as the king was still absent, though expected to arrive at St. James's next day.

The opera over, Charters escorted Sophia to her carriage, and proposed to accompany her home, for he was resolved to remain in a state of suspense no longer. If her rank was so great that she concealed her name from him, why accompany him to the opera, where she was certain of recognition? The mystery was now greater than ever!

On attempting to step into her carriage she said—

"You must not—you cannot come with me—to-night at least."

"Why?" he asked, with surprise.

"The king returns to-morrow from Hanover."

"The king!" repeated Charters, in a bewildered manner. "What has he to do with the love I bear you—the love you have made me so happy by accepting."

"Alas! I cannot tell you here; but we must meet no more," said she, sighing deeply.

The pressure of carriages compelled them to separate. Sophia sank back upon her cushioned seat, and covered her face with her handkerchief, as if she wept bitterly. The heart of Charters was filled with acute sorrow and vague alarm; but could he have seen her fair little face, he would have found it convulsed with—*laughter!*

"Hallo, Charters! so your fair one is gone?" said some one whose voice he recognised; and turning angrily, he found himself face to face with Frederick Shirley, a cornet of his own regiment. "A rare scrape you are in!" the cornet added, with a loud laugh.

"How so, sir?" asked Charters, sharply.

"What on earth tempted you to appear in an opera box with that woman?"

"*That* woman?" he repeated, fiercely; "what woman—who?"

"She who just left you in that absurd turn out—for it *is* absurd—horses, harness, and all," continued the unabashed Shirley; "coronets, plating, and panels."

"Who is she?" asked Charters, somewhat crestfallen.

"What—is it possible that you do not know?" queried Shirley, with an air of utter bewilderment..

"I know that she is adorable, and is called Sophia——"

"Sophia Amelia de Walmoden, Countess of Yarmouth, and bosom friend of his majesty the king!" added Shirley, with another burst of laughter, as he took the arm of Charters and led him away.

Charters was stupified!

He had been thus fooled by the mere mistress of this very unattractive king, some of whose "amorous sallies" in Hanover had excited *her* jealousy, and she was now anxious to revenge herself by exciting his in turn; for she was certain that the Defender of the Faith would hear of her appearance at the opera with a handsome young cavalry officer. So Charters trembled with rage at the thought of his own folly, and began to school himself—however difficult and unpalatable the task—to hate her as much as he had formerly loved her.

Shirley's laughter galled him to the soul at first; but afterwards, over their wine, he showed about a dozen of little pink and peagreen notes, which he had received from his faithless Walmoden, all signed "Sophia."

His appearance in public with the Countess of Yarmouth had given rise to much speculation and gossip in the vicinity of Kensington Palace, and St. James's too; and Shirley was unwise enough to boast frequently of having seen the notes in the possession of Charters; consequently, the latter soon found a secret influence at work against him at headquarters, and that there was little chance of obtaining either a transfer to another corps, or an extension of leave. This was unpleasant, as his funds were so much impaired by extravagance, that he could scarcely rejoin the Dragoon Guards.

While he was in this dilemma, Shirley called at his hotel one morning, and mentioned in confidence, that if he would give up Walmoden's letters, he would find, on looking at the *Gazette*, the position of his affairs materially altered.

Further information he stated himself to be unable, as yet, to afford; so poor Charters, though not of a temper to be threatened even by the king, was scared by the thought of his creditors, and gave up the letters of the Countess to Shirley.

Impatiently he waited for the next *Gazette;* but on opening it, how great was his astonishment and rage to find the following notice:—

"1st Dragoon Guards. Cornet Frederick Shirley to be Lieutenant, *vice* Charters, *who resigns!*"

For some time he could scarcely believe his eyesight. Then he called for his horse and rode to the Horse Guards; but neither the Commander-in-Chief nor the military secretary would receive him, and for weeks he remained a prey to despair and mortification. He sought in vain for the perfidious Shirley, who kept sedulously out of his way, and had now left London.

"My commission, the pride of my heart, was gone," said Charters with a sigh, as he concluded his story; "and by my own folly and extravagance, together with the active assistance of others, my fortune was nearly gone too. Friends disappeared as my purse emptied, and ere long I knew not what to do, or whither to turn me.

"As for Shirley, my lieutenancy availed him but little, as he was dismissed from the service soon after for declining to *go out* with a brother officer. Gradually he became a gambler, a blackleg—in fact, a common robber in London, and his fate was a fearful one; so in my heart, I now forgive him.

"Was he executed?" I inquired.

"Worse. His brother, Sir Jasper Shirley, being out of town, at his place in Hants, the household plate was lodged, as usual, at his banker's. It was valuable, for among it was a princely service he had received from the empress-queen when he was our Ambassador at Vienna; and when a sudden order came to the wary old butler, desiring him to get it all out, as Sir Jasper was returning to town, he showed the letter to my ci-devant friend, Fred Shirley, who said 'it was all right, as his brother would be in London to-morrow.'

"The butler, however, still had his secret fears; and after bringing home the plate, borrowed from a friend a bulldog

—a surly and savage brute of great strength and ferocity, which he chained to the chest over night.

"Shortly before daybreak, a dreadful noise was heard in the apartment where the plate lay. Lights were procured—the butler and other servants hurried to the place, and found that a window had been forced by the usual implements of a housebreaker, who lay on the floor dead, but still warm, and in a pool of blood, for his throat and tongue were completely torn out by the fangs of the ferocious dog; and who think you he proved to be? Sir Jasper's younger brother—Frederick Shirley.

"So," added Charters, through his clenched teeth, "so perished he who betrayed me!

"Drinking, gambling, and reckless dissipation among the *condottieri* of London society, soon brought me like the prodigal of old to the husks and the swine trough; till one day, when my better angel triumphed over the evil spirit who had guided me so long, I conceived the idea of endeavouring to regain, by mere force of merit, the commission of which I had been so lawlessly deprived.

"Inspired by this resolution, so consistent with my warm and sanguine temperament, I enlisted in the Scots Greys; but my evil genius still follows me, for I have never got beyond the rank of corporal.

"I am not the man I once was, and may never rise higher. Perhaps I am too reckless, too much soured in temper, and too much of a misanthrope, to deserve a commission, or it may be that the secret vengeance of the king and his devil of a Walmoden, still pursues me even here. I cannot see my future, but, happily,

> "'There is a Providence doth shape our ends,
> Rough hew them how we will.'"

CHAPTER VIII.

HEAD QUARTERS.

HAVING now related how I became a soldier, almost in desperation and misanthropy, I shall soon show how such emotions gave place to better, to braver, and to higher aspirations, fanned by that blessed *hope* which never dies in the heart of youth.

I learned—but not for a long time after this period—that when news of the step I had taken was brought by the sorrowing old Rector to Netherwood, it gave great satisfaction to my worthy grandfather, and still more to my affectionate cousin Tony, who drained a full bumper to the health of the Frenchman whose bullet should rid them of me for ever; and then Sir Basil was actually barbarous enough to shake him by the hand and say—

"Zounds! Tony, my boy, you may be heir to my title as well as acres, and die a baronet yet!"

After travelling eighteen miles we reached Rothbury, a quaint old market town of Northumberland, pleasantly situated in a valley overlooked by a lofty ridge of rocks. Our head-quarters were here, but some of our troops were billeted at Bickerton, Caistron, and other townships of the parish.

The Coquet flowed through the town, and every morning one of our first duties was to take our horses there to water, which was done by beat of kettledrum, for as yet the Greys, being Horse Grenadiers, had no brass trumpets.

On the morning after our arrival at Rothbury, I was brought before my commanding officer, Colonel George Preston. Tall, handsome, and venerable in aspect, he was a noble veteran officer, though somewhat of an eccentric character in his way. He was now far advanced in life, and had been from his boyhood in the Scots Greys, having entered the regiment as a kettledrummer in the last years of Queen Anne.

He was a captain at the battle of Val, where, at the head of only thirty Greys, he made so furious a charge upon a great body of French cavalry, that he routed and drove them fairly off the field. He then pulled out his purse, and gave each trooper a ducat with his left hand, for his *right* was so swollen by the vigorous use he had made of his broad sword, that the hilt had to be sawn in two by the regimental armourer before he could be released from it.

Under his old-fashioned scarlet uniform, which was cut somewhat in the mode of Queen Anne's days, he wore a *buff coat*, and this was, no doubt, the last appearance of such a garment in any European army.

He received me gravely but kindly, and said,

"So, boy, you have resolved to become a soldier?"

"Yes, noble sir," said I; for as Charters had informed me, this was then the mode of addressing the commanding officer of a regiment.

"You are very young, and seem somewhat different from the common run of our recruits. Your name is rather uncommon, too. I presume that your parents——"

"They are in their graves. I have

none to advise or regret me—none whom I can regret."

(Did no thought of Poor Ruth arrest this sweeping speech?)

"Good! you are then the best of food for gunpowder. Your age——"

"I am about eighteen, sir."

"You look older than that—in face, especially."

"Sir, those who have undergone such years as I have, frequently do so."

In truth, I looked older than my age. My figure was tall, well formed and developed, while my face had a matured expression, and somewhat resolute aspect, especially about the eyes. Colonel Preston, though a stern man, and a strict disciplinarian, felt a deep interest and pride in his regiment, and thus he narrowly examined every recruit before passing him into the ranks, and every man's name and character there, were graven on his memory.

"I like both your spirit and bearing, boy," said he. "Sixty years ago, I was a poor and penniless lad, so I e'en became a private trooper in the Scots Greys, and behold me now! I am Lieutenant-Colonel of the regiment, and hope, please God, to die a General, and go to my grave under a salute of cannon. Ere long, my lads," he continued to me, and several other recruits, who had just been ushered into the Orderly room, "we must all be in France or Germany, and there we shall find what the fortune of war has in store for us. Remember that the sword of a brave man is always sharp, but that of a coward for ever wants grinding! Stand by me, my lads, and I shall never fail you, and in me you see a living example of the reward that may await sobriety, steadiness, and a strict obedience to orders. Put Basil Gauntlet into Captain Lindsay's troop; attach the rest to Captain Cunninghame's. The tailor and the rough-rider will soon make dragoons of them all."

I was conducted to my billet. Fortunately it was in the same tavern where Kirkton and Charters were quartered, and with them I shared the first instalment of my pay, which at that time was small enough, when a cornet had but a half-crown per diem, and a lieutenant-colonel of Dragoons only eight shillings and sixpence!

My bounty-money was soon dissipated, for under pretence of fraternising with me, or teaching me many matters that might be useful, several of those rogues who are usually known in barracks as "old soldiers," or "knowing ones," stuck close to me and to the other recruits, so long as our cash lasted.

The next day saw me arrayed in full uniform. The largest mirror in the tavern (it measured only six inches each way) by no means afforded me sufficient scope for the admiration of my own person in this new attire; though I could view it, when reflected at full length, in the shop-windows, while passing along the streets, into which I at once issued, as Kirkton said, "to exhibit my war-paint."

In those days—this was in the year before we fought at Minden—the Greys wore double-breasted scarlet coats, lined with blue, having slit sleeves; long slashed pockets were in each skirt, and a white worsted aiguilette dangled from the right shoulder. We wore long jack-boots, and tall grenadier caps, with the Scottish Thistle and circle of St. Andrew in front.

Our cloaks were scarlet lined with blue shalloon, and in front they had rows of large flat buttons set two and two, on white frogs, or loops of braid. On our collars we wore a grenade in memory that at its formation, a portion of the regiment had been armed with that formidable weapon, the same as the Scots Horse Grenadier Guards.

Everywhere the proud motto of the corps met my eye; on the standards and kettledrums, on our caps, carbines, and pistol-barrels, and on the blades of our long straight broadswords, I read the words—

SECOND TO NONE!

That short sentence seemed full of haughty spirit; it gave me a new life, and fired my heart with lofty inspirations. I repeated it, dreamed and pondered over it, and as our departure for the seat of war was daily looked for, I longed for active service, and for the peril and adventure ever consequent thereto.

The brusque manners, rough words, oaths and expletives used by some of my comrades, certainly shocked and somewhat blunted my chivalry. To be sure all gentlemen then swore to their hearts content: and I am sorry to say the army carried the fashion to an extreme, and there a quiet fellow was sure to be mocked and stigmatized as a methodist or quaker.

In all the many wars which succeeded its first formation, when it was raised by Sir Thomas Dalyell and Graham of Claverhouse, in 1678, to fight against the hapless covenanters, our regiment had borne a great and glorious part. At the battle of Drumclog and at Airsmoss where Richard Cameron the field-preacher fell, the Greys were, unhappily, the terror of their own countrymen; and even now, after the lapse of so many generations, traditions of those dark days still lingered in our ranks—handed orally down from veteran to recruit.

In better times they had served in the wars of Anne and of the earlier Georges, and always with honour, for in every campaign they captured a colour, and at the battle of Ramilies surrounded and disarmed the French Regiment du Roi, capturing no less than *seventeen standards.**

Our officers were all gentlemen of high spirit, who belonged to the best families in Scotland; and so attached were their men to them, that the corps seemed to be but one large family. Punishments—

* Fact: *vide* "Regimental Record."

especially degradations—were almost unknown; yet "auld Geordie Buffcoat," as they named Preston, was one of the most strict colonels in the service.

Every regiment has its own peculiar history and traditions, just as a family, a city or a nation have; these are inseparably connected with its own honour, achievements and badges, and with the military glory of the country, and thus inspire and foster the fine sentiment of *esprit du corps.*

But to resume:—

We marched southward by easy stages, and during the spring of the year were quartered at Newmarket, where the inns have ever been proverbial for the excellence of their stabling and other accommodation, and whére the race-ground and extensive heath were so admirably adapted for training the cavalry, who were all subjected to severe drill in anticipation of foreign service.

By this time I had gone from squad to squad, rapidly through all the phases which a recruit has to pass—position-drill and sitting up till my spinal column was erect as a pike; club-exercise to expand the chest and strengthen the muscles of the arm. Then came pacing and marching; then equitation, embracing all the skilful and ready aids by which to guide and control my horse in all his paces, and to acquire a firm seat in every variety of movement—to govern him also by my legs and bridle hand, so as to leave my right at the fullest liberty for the use of my weapons. Then I had the exercise of the latter to acquire—the sword, carbine, and pistol. Other hours were devoted to lance, post, and stick practice. Even a smattering of farriery was not omitted; so the first six months which followed my *début* as a Scots Grey left me little leisure for reflection, or for the study of ought else than would conduce to make me a perfect dragoon, skilled in all the science of destroying human life. I learned, moreover, that a *perfect* dragoon is not made in a day.

Colonel Preston daily superintended in person the training of his recruits; and the presence of the fine old man, with his mingled kindness and enthusiasm, kindled a kindred spirit even in the breast of the dullest fellow among us.

It seemed to me—but it might be fancy—that he took particular interest in myself, for he frequently spoke to me with such words of encouragement or praise, that my young heart swelled with gratitude; and I felt certain when the time came, that I would follow the brave old man, even to the cannon's mouth, with the devotion of a son, rather than the mere obedience of a soldier.

An anecdote of our veteran colonel, then current, related that when George II., who frequently displayed much favour and partiality for the Greys (notwithstanding his hatred of the Scots), was reviewing them in Hyde Park one day before the Marshal Duke de Broglie and a prince of the House of Bourbon, Louis Philippe, Duke of Orleans, he said—

"Monseigneur le Prince, did you ever see a finer regiment?"

"They are fine indeed," replied the Prince, as the royal staff passed along the line; "but pardon me if I think them inferior to our Gendarmes de la Garde. Did your majesty ever see *them?*"

"No," replied the king; "but I have

little doubt that my Scots Greys have—eh, Colonel Preston?"

"Yes," said the Colonel, grimly, "we *have* seen them."

"Where?" asked Louis Philippe.

"At Dettingen, when auld Jamie Campbell, who was killed at Fontenoy, led us to the charge against them."

"Well—well," said the king, impatiently, "and what followed?"

"We cut them to pieces, and there I took their *white standard*, cleaving the bearer down to the breeks; and the prince, if he chooses, may see it now, hanging in Westminster Hall."

At Newmarket my chivalry received a severe shock, by being present at the execution of a Light Dragoon who was shot for desertion. He had been sentenced to three hundred lashes by a regimental court-martial. On this, he appealed to a general court, which, instead of confirming the former sentence, inflicted the penalty of—death!

It was long before I forgot the horrors of that scene; the grey light of the early morning—our pale faces on parade—the ominous silence—the almost whispered words of command—the pallid prisoner, as he knelt beside his black deal coffin, and the shriek with which he fell within it as the death volley rang across the far extent of the open heath, and then the trumpet sounding to form open column and pass the poor corpse by files, announced that all was over.

CHAPTER IX.

MY HOPE FOR THE FUTURE.

I HAVE stated that I was placed in the troop of Captain Francis Lindsay, which for a time separated me from my friends, Charters and Kirkton. This was one of the nine troops of Light Horse, or Hussars, lately formed, one of which had been added to every regiment of heavy cavalry.

In a speech recently made in Parliament, His Majesty observed "that the late success of his ally in Germany had given a happy turn to his affairs, which it would be necessary to improve."

The loyal Commons took the hint and liberally granted new supplies, both for the service of Frederick of Prussia, who was then at hostilities with the French monarch, and for enabling the army in Hanover to co-operate with him vigorously; and war having two years before been declared against France, an expedition—of which we were to form part—was prepared for a descent upon the coast of that country.

We were detached from the regiment, and ordered from Maidenhead to Southsea Common, where we were encamped and brigaded with the light troops of other dragoon corps, for instruction in the Prussian exercise; and I may state without vanity that the light troop of the Greys in aspect, mount, and discipline, were allowed by those who saw them far to excel every other in the camp.*

"The *flower* of the Hussars is the troop commanded by Captain Lindsay, quartered at Maiden-

Resolved to rise in the service by my own merit alone, I strained every energy to become master of my drill in all its principles and theory. The sword or foil was never out of my hand when I could find an antagonist; thus I became an expert swordsman, as well as an excellent horseman, and a decidedly good average shot with pistol or carbine. With either, I would put a bullet through a common playing card, when passing it on the ground at full gallop. This devotion to my profession, and my rapid progress did not fail to recommend me to Captain Lindsay, a brave and high-spirited officer,

head, where they have been practising the Prussian exercise, and for some days have been digging large trenches and leaping over them; also leaping high hedges with broad ditches on the other side. Their captain on Saturday last swam his horse over the Thames and back again, and the whole troop were yesterday to swim the river."—*Weekly Journal, May* 23, 1758.

to whom we were all devoted. He was a handsome fellow too, and generous as a prince—to use a common phrase—especially when on service, sharing whatever he possessed with his men.

It was while here under canvas, working hard, drilling, trenching and ditching, teaching myself and my horse—a noble grey, sixteen hands high, and a model of temper and courage—to swim when fully accoutred, that in a tavern near the camp, an old, tattered, and liquor-stained copy of the "Weekly Journal" one evening fell in my way. Books, periodicals, and papers were then almost unknown in camp and barracks, though the gallant General Wolfe had striven hard to encourage the formation of regimental libraries, and since I had donned the red coat, I had neglected everything connected with literature, save a French grammar, of which during my scanty leisure hours, or when on guard, I laboured hard to make myself master.

While lingering over a pint of beer, I read every word of the "Journal," even to the obituary; and in the column of the latter, was a notice that gave me a shock, as if struck by a bullet.

It recorded the death of my grandfather four months ago by a sudden attack of gout in the head, caused, it was stated, by the grief he experienced on hearing that his well-beloved heir, Mr. Anthony Gauntlet, had been killed by a fall from his horse when riding furiously near Kirk Yetholm. "Thus," continued the paper, "the estates of Netherwood, worth thirty thousand per annum, pass to Mr. Anthony's only sister, the charming Miss Aurora Gauntlet, who becomes one of the richest heiresses on the Border, and thus disappears one of our oldest baronetcies, the first Sir John Gauntlet of that ilk, having been one of those, *infeft* in lands in Canada with power of castle, pit and gallows, in the usual form, by the earth and stone of the castle hill of Edinburgh, and by the hand of Charles I., in person, in 1633."

"Disappears!" I muttered, through my clenched teeth. "True, the title disappears; but only for a time I trust."

I sat long buried in thought after this. Thirty thousand pounds per annum! That money by right was mine; this cousin, this Aurora, whom I had never known, never seen, and whom I hated in my heart as a fresh usurper, would doubtless be married by some one—a fortune-hunter, a needy adventurer perhaps—and thus my patrimony would go to the enrichment of strangers, while I——

Thick and fast, fierce thoughts crowded upon me; I had little more than enough to pay for the poor glass of beer I had drunk, but I threw it on the table, and walked sullenly off without waiting for the change.

As I walked along the road, other emotions came over me—emotions that were prouder, better, more lofty and more soothing, for I saw the white tents of the camp—my new home—shining in the setting sun, as they dotted all Southsea Common.

I remembered the story of one whose fate was somewhat, if not exactly, similar—the poor Scottish baronet, Sir Robert Innes, who became a private in the foot regiment of Colonel Winram, of Liberton, and remained there long in obscurity, as private Robert Innes, till a former frien recognised him when on duty as sentinel one day before the quarters of the colonel.

On discovering that he was thus honoured by having a baronet to guard his door, Winram obtained Innes a commission, and gave him in marriage his only daughter and heiress, Margery. I thought I would strive to be like him, and until the lucky spoke of Fortune's wheel turned upmost, I would relinquish, save in my secret heart, all pride of birth or position of family, and the past, and forget too the important monosyllable, of which my unnatural grandfather had left nothing undone to deprive me. This was a brilliant bit of romance, no doubt, but unlike Winram, poor old Colonel Preston had no inheritance save his sword and his quaint uniform; and no beautiful daughter to bestow. I had no former friends to recognise me, and bring about a striking denouement, so I might be sentinel at his door for a hundred years before he could befriend me as Sir Robert Innes was befriended by Colonel Winram.

As a supplement to the notice I had seen, next day on parade the trumpet-major of the Light Horse, who usually acted as our postman, handed me a large thick letter. It bore the Berwick post-mark, and was addressed in the familiar handwriting of Mr. Nathan Wylie.

My heart sprang to my lips, but I had only time to thrust the missive into one of my holsters, for the trumpets sounded to "fall in" and I was kept in an agony of suspense and anxiety to learn the contents—which seemed rather bulky—during the whole of a long and tedious morning parade, with its subsequent drill on the common.

What could this letter be about, what

its contents? Money? It seemed too hard for bank-notes. Was it about Ruth—poor little Ruth whose soft image now rose so upbraidingly before me; for sooth to say, in the hurly-burly of camp and quarters, I had quite forgotten her.

The moment parade and drill were over, I rushed away to a quiet nook, and tore the packet open. It contained a letter from Nathan Wylie, short, dry, and professional, together with an old parchment, snuff-coloured by time.

It briefly stated that in his last will and testament, my respected grandfather had cut me off with the sum of one shilling sterling, which the writer herein inclosed, together with a document which he sent, doubtless as a taunt upon my private's uniform—the diploma of the Netherwood baronetcy.

CHAPTER X.

THE FRENCH DESERTERS.

Lord Anson, Vice-Admiral of the Red, having put to sea with seventeen sail of the line (one of these was the hapless *Royal George*, which afterwards sunk in Portsmouth harbour), and several frigates, with some smaller craft, to block up Brest, and favour the descent to be made on the French coast, our expedition was prepared with great rapidity, and Charles Spencer, Earl of Sunderland, who had lately succeeded to the Dukedom of Marlborough, arrived in camp, to take command of the troops.

Our recent successes by land and sea,

the territories and victories won by our armies in America, the East and West Indies; the almost daily processions through the streets of London, escorting Spanish treasure to the Tower or to the Mint, accompanied by the captured ensigns of French and Spanish admirals, gradually filled all Britain with a fiery enthusiasm, and fanned the passion of glory in the usually phlegmatic breast of John Bull to such a degree, that nothing now was talked of but war and conquest, and the strange resolution was come to of carrying hostilities into the heart of France!

There were mustered on Southsea Common, sixteen regiments of the line, nine troops of Light Horse (ours included) six thousand marines, and three companies of artillery, the whole under the Duke of Marlborough, with Lieutenant-Generals

Lord George Sackville, and William, Earl of Ancrum, K.T., with four Major-Generals, Dury, Mostyn, Waldegrave, and Elliot, the future Lord Heathfield, and "Hero of Gibraltar," who led the Light Horse, six hundred in number.

The noble harbour of Portsmouth, which is so deep and so sheltered by high land that the largest ships of the line may there ride out the roughest storm without touching the ground even at the lowest ebb of the tide, presented a scene of unusual bustle and preparation.

It was crowded by craft of every description; ships of the line, frigates, gun-brigs, tenders, store-ships, and transports; its waters being literally alive with man-of-war boats, barges, and launches, skimming to and fro, filled with seamen and marines, or laden with stores, water-casks, and ammunition which were being conveyed from the town or arsenals to the fleet.

Twelve flat-bottomed boats, each capable of holding sixty-three men, were prepared. These were to be rowed by twelve oars each, and were not to draw more than two feet of water. Meanwhile a vast number of scaling ladders, sandbags to form batteries, baskets for fascines, waggons for the conveyance of wounded, of stores and plunder, had been brought to Portsmouth from the Tower.

Several launches and many bridges, each sixty yards in length, together with floats and stages, for landing the troops, horses, and horse artillery, were made in all haste.

Nothing was omitted that might ensure the success of this daring expedition, for which the departure of Lord Anson's fleet to Brest was certain to open the way, as we had long since swept the fleet of France from the seas; and so great was the enthusiasm in London, that Viscount Downe, Sir John Armytage, Sir James Lowther, and many other English gentlemen of distinction joined the fleet and army to serve as private volunteers.

And there, amid that bustling scene in Portsmouth harbour, lay the *Monarque*, on the quarter-deck of which, the brave Admiral Byng had been judicially murdered, in the preceding year, not as his sentence had it, "for an error in judgment," but to cloak the errors of a ministry!

The infantry destined to serve on our expedition, were three battalions of the Foot Guards; the Eighth, or king's regiment; the famous Twentieth, or Kingsley's; the Welsh Fusileers; the Edinburgh regiment; the Twenty-fourth; Thirtieth; Thirty-third; Thirty-fourth; Thirty-sixth,

Sixty-eighth, and the regiments of Richmond and Talbot.

From Southsea Common the whole force was ordered to the Isle of Wight, where for a short time a camp was formed; but on the same night that the order for this movement was issued, I was despatched on duty to London, bearer of a letter from Commodore Howe to the Lords of the Admiralty.

I knew not what its contents were then, but departed on my mission with the document in my sabretasche, my orders being simply to deliver it at the Admiralty office, and to bring back the answer without a moment of delay. I shall now proceed to relate how I was personally concerned in the contents of the document entrusted to me for delivery.

From the day I joined the army, I was full of eagerness to bring myself prominently before my leaders; but my first essay was singularly unfortunate in its sequel.

One evening when on duty as sentry on foot with my carbine, posted near some sea-stores that were piled on the beach, not far from Southsea Castle, I observed two men of a foreign and somewhat suspicious aspect, who were loitering near, and observing with unmistakeable interest the shipping in the harbour, the distant camp on the common, and the stores that were piled near the castle-gate. On perceiving that I observed them they came directly up to me, and touched their hats with great politeness.

"Mon camarade," said one, in very good French, "we are French sailors——"

"Then you have no business to be loitering here," said I, bluntly and hastily.

"Pardonnez-moi, camarade; but we cannot help it."

"Then you are prisoners of war?"

"Nay——" stammered the other."

"What then?"

"Deserters," was the candid response.

"You are very rash to be here at such a time."

"We have escaped from the castle of St. Malo, where we were shamefully treated, and are anxious to offer our services and our knowledge of the coast."

"To us?"

"*Oui—mon brave*," said the fellow, with a grimace.

"Against your own country?"

"Sacre! our country deserves nothing better at our hands," he continued, smiling and bowing.

My disgust was so strong that I felt tempted to club my carbine and knock the traitor down: but I restrained the emotion and said—

"I am only a private dragoon, and can in no way assist you—so please to move off. It is contrary to orders for me to converse thus, and for you to loiter here."

"We are aware of that," said one, in a deep, growling voice, who had not yet spoken; "but monsieur will perhaps direct us to whom we can apply."

"If you have been in the French Marine service, you should know that well enough yourself."

I paused, and then thinking that, though these men were traitors and rascals, their services or information might be valuable to the general and commodore, I said—

"Messieurs, I may be able to assist you, when relieved from guard. What are your names?"

"Mine is Theophile Damien," said the first speaker.

"And mine, Benoît Bossoit."

"We have both been seamen, and have served on board the privateer ship, *le Maréchal Duc de Belleisle*, under the famous M. Thurot, in that battle off the Firth of Forth, with your two frigates, the *Solebay* and *Dolphin*, in May last."

Next day, when relieved from guard, I met those men, by appointment, at a quiet tavern, where we had some wine, for which they paid liberally, seeming to be very well furnished (especially for deserters) with Louis d'ors; and in the course of conversation I spoke freely—far too freely—of the number, strength, and probable objects of our expedition.

The name of one of these men—a tall, muscular, dark, and coarse-looking fellow, whose subdued manner belied his savage aspect—struck me as being singular.

"You are named Damien, are you not?" I said to him.

"Theophile Damien—at monsieur's service."

"It seems familiar to me."

"As to the most of Europe," said he, bitterly, and he ground his strong white teeth as he spoke.

"What causes your hatred to your country—this disloyalty to your king?"

"Tudieu! have I not told you that we were slaves—galley slaves—and confined in St. Malo?"

(I find myself in honourable company, thought I.)

"Slaves without a crime," growled Bossoit.

"At least I had no crime," said the

other, "save that I bore the hated name of Damien."

"What," I exclaimed, as a sudden light broke upon me; "are you a kinsman of—"

"Exactly, monsieur, of Robert Francis Damien, you would say—of that unfortunate peasant of Ticuloy, who, in January last year, stabbed King Louis, just as he was stepping into his state coach at Versailles, and so nearly rid France of a tyrant—yes, I am his brother."

"Was not this would-be regicide deranged?" said I, as fresh doubts of the value of such a pilot occurred to me, and I feared for my own honour, if found in company with Frenchmen of such a character, and especially at such a conjecture.

"His reason was wavering—poverty and the long wanderings of an unsettled life had made it so; but instead of confining him in a prison or fortress, he died of the most dreadful tortures," replied the first Frenchman.

"So I have heard."

"The king's wound was slight; but my brother was beaten to the earth by the sword hilt of Guillaume de Boisguiller, a captain of the French Guards, several of whom in the first transports of their zeal and fury, burned him severely with their torches, while he lay prostrate at their feet. A fortnight after this he was tried and tortured. Shall I tell you what followed? *Tête Dieu!* my blood boils, and my heart sickens at the memory of it. After making the *amende honorable* in the Church of Notre Dame, he was conveyed to the Place de Grêve, where vast multitudes were assembled; where every window was filled with eager faces—and every housetop bore a living freight.

"The Provost of the merchants, the Echevins and other magistrates of Paris, in their robes, with all the great lords and ladies of the court, occupied the windows of the gloomy Maison aux Piliers, or Hotel de Ville, on the spire and pavilions of which banners waved as for a festival. In the square, beyond the scaffold and the troops who circled it, scarcely was there breathing space, so closely, so densely were the spectators massed; but a silence like that of death hushed every tongue, for they knew that a scene of horror was about to ensue."

The Frenchman paused; the perspiration stood in bead-drops on his brow; his face was deadly pale, and I could not fail to feel deeply interested, while thinking at the same time, that the language and bearing of himself and his companion were very different from what one might expect to find in a couple of runaway privateersmen.

"If, on that terrible day," he resumed, "voices were heard, it was the murmur of those at a distance—those who were too far off to see—the thousands who crowded the narrow vistas of the Rue de la Tannerie, the Rue de la Mortellarie, the Rue du Mouton, and the Quai de la Grêve, for all Paris had flocked to witness my brother's execution.

"At five o'clock, just as the grey light of a dull March morning stole over the pale-faced multitude, the punishment began. My brother's right hand was half consumed by fire, and then struck off. Amid the agony, though his limb shrivelled and blood burst forth, *O mon Dieu!* the poor soul neither winced nor asked for mercy; but when pincers, red hot and glowing, and ladles filled with boiling oil, molten lead and flaming resin, were applied to his arms, thighs, and breast, he uttered shrieks so piercing that every heart grew sick and every face grew pale. On his bones the very flesh was broiled, and his blood hissed in steam around him! He was then disembowelled."

"Assuredly that must have put a period to his sufferings?" said I, in a low voice.

"No—the principle of life was strong within him, for my poor brother was one of the most athletic of our peasants in Artois. These agonies—this butchery were insufficient to glut the rage of the courtiers and the fury of his judges. Four strong young horses were now harnessed to his four limbs, and lashed in opposite directions, but failed to sever his mangled frame, and he had now ceased to cry or moan."

"Failed, say you?" I exclaimed, becoming more and more interested, in spite of myself, by the Frenchman's detail of this revolting execution.

"Yes—so the chief executioner, with a sharp knife, severed the sinews at the joints of the arms and thighs. Anew, the long whips were cracked—again the horses strained upon their traces, and a leg and arm were torn from the body of my brother, who looked—mother of mercy!—yes, *looked* after them, as they were dragged along the pavement, with the blood spirting from vein and artery; but on the severance of the other two limbs, he expired.

"His remains were then cast into a fire, which was kept burning all day, and all the succeeding night."

"Were you present at this horrible scene?" I asked, after a pause.

"No—I was with Monsieur de Thurot, cruising off the coast of Scotland. On my return to France, I found my brother's family and name, even to the most remote degree, proscribed, and the cottage in which we were all born, at Tieuloy, in Artois, razed to its very foundations in token of infamy, and the place where it stood had been salted and sown with grass. On hearing of all this, some bitter words escaped me, so I was placed in the castle of St. Malo. There I made a vow to achieve both freedom and revenge. I have fulfilled the first part of that vow, and, *Dieu-merci!* I am here."

A peculiar glance, the meaning of which at that time I could not understand, passed between the speaker and his companion; and as the story of the former seemed a strange one, I conducted them at once to Captain Lindsay of our troop.

He questioned them in a manner that displayed considerable contempt for the new character they wished to assume; and then sent them with a note to Commodore Howe, who at once accepted their services, and it was with a dispatch containing some real or pretended information they had given, that I was sent to London, on the evening when the troops began to move for the Isle of Wight; and I departed, happy in heart and high in spirit, furnished with an order to the constables of parishes and others, to furnish me with such relays of horses as I might require.

Four days' pay were given to me in advance; but as I left the camp, Captain Lindsay generously and kindly put a half-guinea in my hand, and desired me to "make myself comfortable, and for the honour of the corps, to avoid all scrapes and doubtful company by the way."

CHAPTER XI.

WANDSWORTH COMMON.

It was a lovely May evening when I left busy Portsmouth. The shadows of the tossing branches of the old limes and sycamores that bordered the wayside were cast far acros the yellow corn; the white and purple lilacs, the golden laburnum trees, and the tall hollyhocks with their gorgeous crimson flowers, made beautiful the gravelled avenues that led to many a villa and farm, while the fertile uplands that sloped in distance far away, were half hidden in the warm haze of the summer sunset.

I felt proud of my showy uniform,

proud of my beautiful grey charger, and proud of the mission on which I was departing, though in the humble capacity of an orderly dragoon; and I was happy in the prospect of two days of perfect freedom from the routine and trammels of the camp, for a soldier, however young and enthusiastic, soon learns that he is no longer "the lord of his own proper person."

My chain bridle and steel scabbard jangled in unison to the clank of my horse's hoofs, as he trotted rapidly along the level highway, and in my young heart swelled anew all the pride of being a soldier, a horseman, and an *armed one.*

Within a week I should probably be treading the soil of hostile France, even as I was then treading the soil of peaceful and happy England. France! might I ever return from thence? Many of us were fated there to find our last home, and might I not be one of the doomed? I thrust aside the thought—not that I feared death, I was too young and too hopeful for that; but shrunk from the idea of perishing with the mass, before I had achieved what I conceived to be my mission; before I had won myself a right to bear with honour the name my forefathers had bequeathed to me, and before I had resumed that title, the diploma of which the miserable Nathan Wylie had sent in mockery to the private soldier!

Night came on and the road grew dark and lonely; there was no light save that of the stars, which I saw reflected at times in the bosom of the Wye, and twelve tolled from the steeples of St. Mary and St. Nicholas, as I entered the quaint old market town of Guildford, and rode straight to the Red Lion, where I stabled my horse and ordered a relay for the morrow.

A forty miles' ride gave me a good appetite; I supped and retired to bed, where I slept without a dream even of the future, for I was weary.

The next day was far advanced before I set forth again; but I proceeded slower now, the hack furnished to me by the innkeeper proving very different in mettle from my fine grey charger. In short, the animal nearly broke down by the way, and though the distance between Guildford and the metropolis is only about thirty miles, evening closed in before I saw at a distance the vast and dusky dome of St. Paul's, rising in sombre grandeur from amid the yellow haze, formed by the smoke and by the myriad lights of London.

I had left behind me the little village

of Wandsworth, which is finely situated on the declivities of two small hills, and was traversing the common, then a wild and open waste covered with grass, gorse, and tall waving weeds through which the roadway passed. Clouds had now obscured the stars, and the night was so dark that I had some difficulty in tracing my path, though the accumulated glare of the innumerable street lamps and other lights of the vast city was very distinct but a few miles off, rendering the foreground darker.

When about the middle of the common, I heard the sharp report of a pistol and then the scream of a woman. These alarming sounds, and the flash of the explosion, came from the very path I had to traverse, so I spurred on my jaded hack, and found a carriage stopped on the common by two armed and mounted highwaymen, with crape masks on their faces. Such gentry were at that period still in the zenith of their perilous fame.

They had fired a shot to make the postillion pull up, and were now stationed one at each window of the carriage, demanding the purses and other valuables of the travellers.

My holster pistols were at the demi-pique saddle of my troop horse, which I had left at Guildford; so drawing my sword, I rode boldly up and demanded what was the matter, and who fired the shot I had heard.

"You had better ride on and attend to your own affairs," replied a surly fellow, with a horrible oath, as he coolly reloaded his pistol.

"Surrender your weapon, rascal," I exclaimed, resolutely, "or I shall cut you to the teeth!"

"Fire at him, Bill," cried he to his

comrade. "Zounds! are we both to be cowed by a saucy shoulder-knot?"

On hearing this, his comrade urged his horse furiously round from the other side of the carriage. Then I heard another female shriek as he levelled a bright-barrelled blunderbuss, the bell-muzzle of which was so near my face that the light flashed on it as he drew the trigger, for happily it only burned priming; otherwise my head would have been blown to atoms, as on inspection afterwards I found this formidable firearm was loaded with slugs of lead and iron.

"Hung fire, by all that's infernal!" exclaimed the fellow; but his exclamation of wrath ended in a howl of agony, when by a stroke of my sword I hewed off half of his right hand, and the weapon fell on the road, together with three of his fingers. On this they put spurs to their horses and galloped away at a break-neck pace.

With a shout of victory I pursued them for a few hundred yards across the common, and then returned at a canter to the carriage, the occupants of which proved to be two ladies, who, by their manner and difference of years, appeared to be mother and daughter. They had with them a waiting-maid, and it was she whose cries I had twice heard.

Their air was distinguished; the younger was a very beautiful girl with fair hair and a delicate complexion, but this was all I could discern by the light of a carriage lamp, which one of the footmen—a rascal who had hitherto hidden himself among some fern—now held within the window, while the ladies were putting on their rings, gloves, and bracelets which they had drawn off to surrender at the moment I came so luckily to their rescue.

"Mamma, dear mamma, all danger is past. They are gone, and we are safe; be assured, be satisfied," I heard the soft voice of the younger say imploringly to the elder, who was excessively agitated.

"Ladies," said I, touching my cap, "be composed now, I pray you; those fellows have fled, and are not likely to return. Fortunately, I have put a mark upon one that he will not easily efface."

"Sir," replied the elder lady, in a voice still tremulous with alarm, "accept our deepest gratitude. To you we owe our rescue. Our money and jewels would have been a trifling loss, but how know we that these men might not have murdered us here on this lonely heath? and we hear of such dreadful things in these days."

"But was your servant here without pistols?"

"No, a pair of loaded horse-pistols are always in the rumble with John," replied the young lady.

"Why did you not use them, fellow?" said I, turning sharply to the valet.

He reddened and stammered something about the danger or rashness of one man encountering two, but his knees were trembling under him, and the hand which held the carriage lamp shook as if with palsy. In fact, he seemed so convulsed with fear that the young lady and I could not forbear laughing at him.

"When passing this way again, I shall take care to travel by daylight, or with a bolder escort than you, John Trot," said she, while the maid-servant, whose face I had not yet seen, as she sat in a dark corner, loudly and bitterly expressed her contempt for the unfortunate knight of the shoulder-knot, and for his lack of valour.

"We left the residence of a friend near Croydon about sunset, and should have been in London long since," observed her mother, "but a wheel came off at the cross road which leads to Kingston, and thus we were detained until this unpleasant hour. Have you, sir, also come from Croydon?"

"Nay, madam, I have just come from Portsmouth."

"Portsmouth!" echoed both ladies, with voices expressive of interest and animation.

"With despatches from Commodore Howe for the Lords of the Admiralty," said I, with an emotion of vanity difficult to repress, especially at my age then.

"Are you one of those who are bound for France?"

"Yes, madam."

"When does the fleet sail with the army?"

"Next week, 'tis said; but nothing definite has yet transpired," I replied, with all the air of a staff officer.

"Poor boy!" I heard her say, with something like a sigh, and with winning softness of tone, as the valiant John Trot asked if the carriage was to move on.

"As the night has become so dark, madam," said I, "you must allow me to have the honour of escorting you to town. You have still to pass Clapham Common, and its reputation for safety is somewhat indifferent. Even in Lambeth I have heard that robberies have been frequent of late."

"But how can we trespass so far upon your kindness, sir?" urged the young lady, whose voice made my heart beat faster.

"Believe me, madam, I deem it a great honour and happiness to have been of service to you, and for to-night, at least, your way shall be mine. I am pretty well mounted, and very well armed."

"Fortunately, you are also proceeding to London," said her mother; "therefore I accept your polite offer with gratitude."

I bowed nearly to my horse's mane, and then said to the valet—

"Hand up that blunderbuss, John; it may serve as a trophy, and remind your lady of to-night's engagement on Wandsworth Common."

"And the three fingers—oh—ugh?" asked John, with chattering teeth.

"Those you may pocket, if you please,"

said I, while withdrawing the charge, which, as I have said, proved to be slugs. I put the weapon in the rumble, and then the carriage was driven off.

As it rolled over the dark heath, I rode at a quick trot behind it; but frequently, when our pace became slower as we ascended a slope and the horses walked, the ladies conversed with me, and then I rode abreast of the open windows.

It was evident that by being muffled in my trooper's cloak, and having on a small foraging cap, I was taken for an officer; thus the elder lady gave me her card, and expressed, in the usual polite terms, the delight it would afford them to see me at their residence in some modish square (I failed to catch the name), if I had leisure to-morrow morning, as they had to leave town again at mid-day.

I felt piqued, and an emotion somewhat

of bitterness and mortification stole into my heart; and while secretly cursing alike the rules of society and my own false position, I thanked her for the kind invitation, but without the least intention of availing myself of it. After this, I became a little reserved; but it was a difficult task to be so with the young lady, who was a lovely girl, and lively too. She conversed with me gaily, and asked if I longed for foreign service; if I thought the war would be protracted; if we were sure to beat the French; if I was not afraid—she begged pardon for such a silly question—of being shot in battle; and a hundred other pretty nothings, while her sweet face and sparkling eyes seemed to come out of the gloom of the travelling carriage, and then to fade into it again, as we passed an occasional dim street-lamp, all of which in those bygone days I need scarcely say were lighted by oil.

At the bridge of Westminster, which had been built about ten years before, I bade them adieu, and with something like a sigh of regret, departed in search of some humble hostelry wherein to pass the night.

This brief meeting—the whole episode in all its details interested me deeply. Those women so highly bred, so delicately nurtured, so richly dressed, so gentle and winning in manner, were so different from those whom I was now compelled to meet, in camp and barracks, at the canteen and sutler's tent, that for the first time my heart repined at the prospect before me.

"Pshaw!" said I, "let me think of this no more." But near a lamp I reined up to examine the lady's card, and searched my pockets in vain. I had lost it!

"It matters little," thought I; "and yet, withal, I should like to have known their names." And amid the roar and bustle of the lighted streets of London, I still seemed to hear the merry laugh and gentle voice of the fair-haired girl whose hand I had so recently held in mine.

CHAPTER XII.

THE RACE.

All the adventures of the preceding night appeared but a dream, when early next morning—at least so early as I could hope to find any high officials at their office—I rode through the crowded streets of London, and delivered the despatch of Commodore Howe at the Admiralty.

"Immediate" being written on the envelope, I had to remain in a waiting-room for more than an hour, after which the answer was entrusted to me, addressed, "On H.M. Service," to Commodore Howe. As I afterwards learned from the public prints, this document, among other instructions, empowered him to avail himself of "the services and information of the two French deserters named on the margin—Theophile Damien and Benoit Bossoit."

I consigned it to my sabretasche, remounted, and quitted London at a quick pace about two p.m.

On leaving the greater thoroughfares behind, when traversing the suburbs I easily lost my way, and at a tavern, near which a number of fellows in their shirt-sleeves were playing skittles, I drew up to inquire the way to Portsmouth.

I questioned one who was seated at the door smoking; he was a man with a very sullen and forbidding expression of face, who had his left hand thrust into the breast of his vest. He wore a shabby snuff-coloured suit with large steel buttons; his legs were incased in long riding-boots spotted with mud, and I perceived the brass butts of a pair of pistols, peeping from his square flapped side pockets.

I was somewhat surprised when this sinister-looking stranger, after giving me a long and ferocious stare, started from his seat, uttered a deep imprecation, and entered the house. I then called to the skittle players, and repeated my question to them.

On this they simultaneously abandoned their game, and gathered about me.

"The Portsmouth road lies straight before you," said one; "be you going to France, my lad?"

On my replying in the affirmative, they gave a simultaneous cheer, and, amid cries of "Old England for ever!" and "Down with the Johnny Crapauds!" I had to drink with them all, and they continued to wave their hats as long as I was in sight, while galloping along the road they had indicated.

Being anxious to reach Portsmouth and to rejoin, I rode at a hard trot; the road was good, the country open and level. Two mounted persons appeared at times behind me; but I continued to keep in advance of them. Some association of ideas made me think of the sulky fellow I had seen at the tavern door, and of the two highwaymen of the preceding night; but after a time I perceived that one of the riders was a lady, and that both were coming along at a rasping pace, as if determined not to be distanced and left behind by me.

I had taken the Epsom road, thus a ten miles' ride brought me to Ewell, near which, in a pleasant green lane, where the plum and apple trees that bordered the way intertwined their branches overhead

—one of those quiet, dewy, and shady green lanes that are so peculiarly English, where the bees hum, and the gossamer webs are spun—I drew bridle to breathe my horse.

I now heard the sound of hoofs coming rapidly along the road, and in a minute after, there swept past me the fair traveller I had seen, and some yards behind her rode a man in livery. They were both admirably mounted on blood horses. Her ample skirt, her long fair hair, and the ostrich plume in her hat streamed behind her. I could see with a glance that she had her horse well in hand, though it flew almost at racing speed, causing mine to rear and strain upon the bit, as she passed me with a merry ringing laugh of delight, and with a flourish of her whip, so much as to say, "A challenge—we have distanced you at last!"

This I was not slow in understanding, and feeling somewhat piqued, put spurs to my nag, and dashed off in pursuit by the highway that led to Epsom.

Twice I saw her looking back, which her valet, though a good horseman, scarcely dared to do; and each time she plied her little riding-switch with no very sparing hand, and like a girl of spirit.

Copsewood in full foliage, thatched cottages half buried among ivy, hops and flowers, ripe corn fields, and red brick houses, seemed to fly past, and in a very short space we found ourselves traversing Banstead Downs. I gained on them fast, for my horse had been thoroughly breathed. I soon passed the livery servant, and a few more bounds brought me neck and neck with his mistress, who turned to me laughingly, a flush—the genuine flush of youth, pleasure, and exercise glowing in her soft cheek—and simultaneously we pulled in our horses on recognising each other.

She was the charming blonde I had met on Wandsworth Common—the heroine of my last night's adventure!

My cavalry cloak was rolled and strapped to my saddlebow; and I thought there could be no mistaking my private's uniform now, and indeed, her countenance changed very perceptibly as she said, half breathlessly—

"Good morning, my friend. So I have actually been running away from the person to whose courage mamma and I owe so much!"

"It would almost seem so," said I, bowing.

"Believe me, sir, I knew not that it was you," she resumed, colouring deeply, and casting down her eyes (how fair her soft loveliness looked by day!). "I saw but a horseman before me, and could not resist the temptation of passing him."

"Nor could I resist the desire of accepting your very palpable challenge," I replied, just as the valet came up, fearfully blown, and in his crimsoned face I recognised the features of the valiant Mr. John Trot.

"But I was not altogether trying a race with you," said the young lady, still blushing deeply, and beginning to move her horse away; "I was riding fast to overtake mamma, who is in yonder carriage. She is come to drink the waters of Ashted Spa, and I doubt not will be glad to tender you once again her thanks."

With these words, and with an air that seemed to say, "This interview, or this mistake, has lasted long enough," she bowed and urged her horse towards the carriage, which was standing about fifty paces distant on the high road, and from a window of which I saw a lady observing us.

The young girl's figure showed to perfection on horseback, and her riding-habit, which was of light green cloth, trimmed with narrow gold braid, suited well her blonde beauty and golden-coloured hair. She wore a broad black beaver hat, from which a single ostrich feather drooped gracefully on her left shoulder. Loosened by the roughness of the gallop, her soft hair flowed over her neck in silky ripples—I know no more fitting term—of light golden brown, that glittered in the sunshine. Her riding-gauntlets were of yellow leather, and her hands, as they grasped the reins and riding-switch, seemed small, compact, and beautifully formed.

"I thought we had lost you, madcap!"

said her mamma, with annoyance in her tone and manner; "what caused you to gallop thus along the Downs, as if riding a race?"

"I was running something very like it, certainly, mamma; but do you not see that we have been overtaken by—the—the gentleman who saved us from robbery last night?"

"I am hastening back to Portsmouth, madam," said I, with a profound salute. "In my ignorance of the country I have taken the road to Epsom instead of that which leads to Cobham, and to this mistake I owe the good fortune of meeting with you again."

"You had not time, probably, to visit us before leaving town this morning?" said she.

"I had the mischance, madam, to lose your card."

At that moment, a man of sinister aspect, and shabbily attired, but with holsters at his saddle, looked fixedly at us, as he rode slowly past, on a bald-faced bay horse.

His *left* hand was bound up by a red handkerchief, and, consequently, he held the reins of his bridle with the *right*. He glared at me, with a glance of such undisguised ferocity, that I had not a doubt he was the wounded rascal of last night's adventure—the same man, he of the snuff-coloured suit and steel buttons, whom I had seen with the skittle players in the suburbs of London.

Was he dogging me?

If so, 'twere well to be prepared. All this flashed upon my mind with the usual rapidity of thought; but I was too much interested by my new friends to attend to him then, and, ere our interview was over, he had disappeared upon the way to Guildford—the road *I was to pursue.*

"Zounds! I must look out," thought I, "or there may be a blank in Lindsay's muster-roll to-morrow."

CHAPTER XIII.

THE HANDKERCHIEF.

"It is, indeed, singular that we should meet again, and so soon, too!" said the elder lady, who, notwithstanding the silver tinge amid her auburn hair, still bore unmistakable traces of a beautiful person; "your regiment is, I think, a Horse Grenadier one?"

"Yes, madam."

"The Guards?"

"No—it is the Scots Greys, or Second Dragoons—yet we boast ourselves 'Second to None.'"

"A proud vaunt," said she, smiling at my manner.

She was silent for a few moments, during which I was conscious that her daughter was observing me with some interest. As our officers did not then wear epaulettes, but simply a silver aiguilette, her next observation was an awkward one for me.

"You are a captain, I hope?" said she, smiling.

"Nay—I am too young," I replied, with a hesitating manner and a glowing cheek.

"Yet Wolfe, whom I once knew, was a colonel at twenty. Then you are a cornet?"

I felt the blood rushing to my temples—yet wherefore should I have blushed "for honest poverty?"

"Curiosity is the privilege of our sex," said the young lady, coming to my rescue; "thus mamma is most anxious to know to whose bravery we owed our safety."

"Madam, I have not the honour to be more than a private trooper," said I, with a bearing of pride that had something stern in it.

Mamma did not lose her presence of mind, though the colour in her daughter's cheeks grew deeper, but replied—

"Ah, indeed! I believed you by your bearing to be an officer." She drew her head within the carriage.

"I thank you, madam; I was not always what I am to-day," said I, sadly.

"And now, my good fellow, if you will favour me with your name, Colonel Preston shall be duly informed, by letter, of your courage."

There was another pause, during which I shortened my reins, and was turning my horse, when the winning voice of her daughter, which had a singularly sweet chord in it, arrested me, as she said—

"You belong, you state, to the Greys?"

"Yes."

"Do you know a soldier named Gauntlet—Basil Gauntlet?"

It was now *my* turn to feel confusion and extreme surprise.

"Yes; but how has he the honour, the happiness to be known to you?" I inquired, with growing astonishment, while gazing into her clear, bright eyes.

"I have an interest—have we not *both* an interest in him, mamma?" said she, with confusion.

"You—in a poor unfriended trooper?" I exclaimed.

"He is from our neighbourhood—that is all," replied the young lady, with a hesitating manner.

I scanned her face in vain; its soft expression and lovely features, her hair of golden-brown, her eyes of dark blue-grey—eyes full of faith, of truth and merriment withal, were quite unknown to me, and my heart beat quicker while my bewilderment increased, as she said—

"We have heard that this ill-starred lad has become wild, rakish, bad, incorrigible and ugly."

"Ugly? Come, I am sorry you say so," said I, with something of pique.

"Why?" asked the mamma, raising her eyebrows and eyeglass.

"Gauntlet and I are alike as twin brothers could be, and I don't like to hear him reviled."

"Ah, indeed," said she, glancing at me leisurely through her eyeglass. Then, as thoughts of Jack Charters' countess, and the scrape *she* had lured him into occurred to me, I resolved to become reserved; but could not help inquiring—

"Permit me, ladies, to ask how poor Gauntlet is so fortunate as to interest you?"

"We are namesakes—that is all," replied the elder lady, rather coldly.

"Namesakes!" echoed I; but at that moment, as the arms on the panel of the carriage door caught my eye—a shield *argent* charged with a gauntlet *gules*—a new light broke upon me. Anger—sudden, fierce, and glowing anger—was my next impulse, and, turning to the fair rider, I stammered, but my voice almost failed me, "You are—you are——"

"The granddaughter of Sir Basil Gauntlet, of Netherwood," said she, with haughty surprise.

I was silenced and confounded! This lovely girl whom I had twice met so singularly and so abruptly, was my cousin Aurora, the new usurper of my patrimony—one whom I had schooled myself to hate and in my soul revile; and this elder lady, so noble, so courtly, and still so handsome, was the mother of my late fox-hunting cousin Tony—my aunt by marriage—she who doubtless believed me to be—if she ever thought of me at all—the outcast, runaway, and worthless wretch my unnatural grandfather had sought to make me.

Pride and a just sense of indignation swelled up within me, and I sat on my horse, silent, irresolute, and stern. Aurora and her mother knew little of the stormy, the fierce conflict of nameless emotions that raged in my heart.

"Adieu, soldier," said the mamma, "with a thousand thanks for the service so bravely and politely rendered. If you will not give us your name, at least do me the favour of accepting this," she added, drawing forth her—*purse*.

I uttered a scornful laugh, and reining back my horse, said—

"Nay, nay, ladies, though impoverished and humbled, I cannot submit quietly to the degradation of being offered money."

"This is most singular!"

"How is mamma to reward you?" asked the young lady, with something of surprise and, as I thought, pleasure in her tone. It might be that I flattered myself.

"By permitting you to give, and me to accept—" said I, taking a lace handkerchief from her hand, for I was always a lover of effect, and resolved to produce one now —"of this trifle as a remembrance——"

"Of what?" she asked, blushing to the temples; "a remembrance of what?"

"That Basil Gauntlet has been of some

service to Aurora, the beautiful cousin who has done him a grievous wrong in unwittingly depriving him of his heritage and birthright. Three days, now, may find me on the seas for France; so adieu, aunt and cousin, adieu for evermore!"

Then I cut short this remarkable interview by spurring my horse with such energy that he made a wild bound, and sprang away at a dashing pace along the road to Guildford.

Impulse had made me take Aurora's handkerchief, and impulse now made me regret having done so.

Pride resumed its sway, and thus, while riding furiously along the road, I never turned once to look behind me.

CHAPTER XIV.

THE RED LION AT GUILDFORD.

As I rode on, anger, pride, a keen sense of the foul injustice with which my family had treated me, and of the false position in which they had placed me with the world, prompted me with a desire to cast Aurora's handkerchief to the wind; but the knowledge that *she* was an unwitting participator in the act by which my grandfather had transferred my heritage to her late brother, Tony; the memory of her kind manner, the gentle expression of her eye; together with certain high-flown ideas I had gathered from novels, tales of chivalry, and other romantic lore, prompted me to retain it. Edged with lace, it was of the finest cambric, and "Aurora," marked by her own hand, no doubt, appeared on one of its corners.

It was strange, but certainly not unpleasing, that she should think of and ask for me, whom she had never seen; and the tones of her winning voice yet lingered in my ear. My mind soared into airy regions, and became filled with tumultuous and undefined thoughts, for I was a famous architect of castles in the air.

"Ah, that I had the lamp of Aladdin, or even his ring, for ten minutes!" I exclaimed.

Aurora—who was well named so, with her pure complexion and golden hair—was the only living relative who had ever bestowed a thought upon me, so I placed the relic of her in my breast, and rode on, little foreseeing that on a future day that handkerchief would prove the means of saving my life.

On reaching Guildford, I repaired at once to the inn, where, on entering the stable, I remember well how my noble grey welcomed me by neighing, by licking my hand, and rubbing his forehead against me, when I greeted him as an old friend.

In the next stall there was a bald-faced nag with eyes askance, surveying us over the trevice boards, and his aspect seemed familiar to me.

The Red Lion at Guildford was one of those huge, misshapen, queer old galleried houses which still survive the Tudor days in many parts of England. It had acute wooden gables, with stacks of clustered chimneys that started up in picturesque confusion. The walls were plastered and whitewashed, and had varnished beams of ancient oak, in some instances richly and grotesquely carved, placed in them horizontally, perpendicularly, and diagonally. On the side which faced the stable-yard there opened a triple row of bedroom galleries, having twisted balustrades; and all this quaint superstructure rose from an arcade composed of octagonal stone pillars and ponderous beams of good old English oak elaborately carved. Gigs, chaises, covered carts, and red four-wheeled waggons, occupied the sheds around the yard; and the sound of hoofs and the rattle of stall collars evinced that the stables were well filled.

When I arrived night was closing in, and a bright red light streamed cheerily through the windows of the bar into the outer darkness as I entered by the porch, which had a flight of steps down, instead of up to the door, for so old was the edifice that the soil had gradually accumulated far above its original basement.

I am thus particular in describing the house, in consequence of a startling incident which occurred during the few hours I sojourned there.

I inquired of the ostler to whom the bald-faced nag belonged, and he replied to a gentleman who had retired to bed, weary with a long journey.

The host of the Red Lion was so patriotic that he insisted upon having me to sup with him, and he would make no charge for my own or horse's entertainment. He drank deeply, and anon was soon borne away to bed by the ostler and waiter, while shouting vociferously, "Britons, strike home!" and "Down with the Johnny Crapauds!"

After this, I retired immediately, being anxious to reflect a little over the passages of the day, to sleep, and if possible to depart by daybreak.

As the waiter, candle in hand, was conducting me along one of the bedroom galleries, which I have described as overlooking the stable-yard, a dark figure appeared to hover at the further end; and there from amid the shadow a human face seemed to peer out as if observing us.

The hour was late, and the place in all its features strange to me. I stepped towards this eavesdropper, but he or she immediately disappeared.

If ghosts there were in Guildford, the upper regions of the quaint old tumble-down Red Lion seemed to be the very place in which one might take up its quarters, but other thoughts than of ghosts were in my head, so I inquired where the rider, or proprietor of the bald-faced nag was located.

"In number six," replied the waiter.

"On this gallery?"

"Yes, sir."

"And mine?"

"Is number twelve—the oak room. His is at yonder end."

"'Twas there the figure disappeared."

"Figure? Well, there ain't no ghosts or ghostesses either in the Red Lion that ever I heard of, and I have been here both man and boy these many years."

"How is this traveller dressed?" I continued.

"In brown broadcloth, I think, master."

"With a rusty old cocked hat?"

"Yes, bound with black galloon."

"Is his left hand wounded?"

"Don't know," replied the waiter, yawning, "for he keeps it always in his weskit pocket."

My suspicions now amounted to certainty. He was my acquaintance of Wandsworth Common—the highwayman, beyond a doubt. We were certainly in too close proximity, but the landlord of the inn was too tipsy to be referred to, and I had no desire to be detained upon the morrow, charged as I was with important papers for the commodore at Portsmouth, thus I made no more remarks, but took the candle, entered my room, and shut the door.

The apartment was entirely pannelled with dark wainscot, hence its aspect was quaint and gloomy; the furniture was uncomfortably antique, for this being one of the upper and cheaper lodgings of the Red Lion, the whole appurtenances were the oldest in the house, having gradually retired from story to story, till their last service was to be spent in the attics.

The fireplace was wide, lined with blue Dutch tiles, and had a little old-fashioned basket grate, set upon square blocks of stone.

From the latticed window I could see the Wye winding under the bridge, the dark arches of which were clearly reflected in its starlit current beneath.

Two strong bolts secured my door, so there was no danger of being surprised by my friend in the snuff-coloured suit through that avenue. I threw off my belts and uniform, and slipped into a bed that felt cold, damp, and old, for the moths flew out of the russet-coloured canopy and hangings, to flutter about the candle end, the light of which expired just at the moment when I had no further use for it.

I felt feverish, wakeful, and full of many thoughts. Then there were strange sounds in this old house rather calculated to banish sleep; the night wind moaned in the wide chimneys: rats scampered about behind the decaying wainscot, scattering fragments of lime in their career. It might be fancy, but twice some one seemed to lift the latch of my door softly as if attempting to open it.

Ere sleep began to weigh my eyelids down, I had mentally rehearsed over and over again the two unexpected interviews with my cousin Aurora; and again I repented having condescended to take her handkerchief even in a spirit of gallantry.

It was very cavalier-like no doubt—very romantic and all that; but in my heart I linked her and her mother with those who had outraged and wronged me, and pride dictated that I should have left them in ignorance of who I was, and then have ridden off on my lonely way. However, now the deed was done, and regret was unavailing.

Would they—Aurora and her stately mother—triumph over the temporary, alas! it might be permanent, obscurity and humility of my position? There are human hearts wicked enough to feel such triumph, for many persons hate those whom they wrong; but Aurora's gentle voice and tone of sympathy when addressing me removed the supposition that she could be guilty of this.

I had met with so little kindness in the world that the circumstance of her remembering even my existence impressed me deeply.

These two interviews dwelt long in my memory. I was now excluded from the society of polished and educated women: indeed, from the force of that evil destiny to which I had been abandoned, I had hitherto seen little of either; thus the charm of my cousin's manner and the beauty of her person filled my heart with new aspirations, and a keener desire to assume my place in society; but at present the die was cast, and to France must I go as a private dragoon.

My half-drowsy ruminations had been frequently disturbed by sounds too strange to escape my observation. At last they impelled me to sit up in bed, to listen and to look around me.

The room was dark as a tomb, save where through the fantastic iron tracery of the antique window I could see the clouds, like masses of black crape, float past the twinkling stars.

On the wind, which came down the old chimney, there were borne sounds like sobs and sighs—like fierce mutterings and groans that became deep, hollow, and agonizing; and they seemed to be emitted from the wall immediately above the fire-place.

My ears tingled and drops of perspiration started to my forehead, for I must confess that, at the moment, I was weak enough to fear the supernatural, until there came the decidedly earthly sound of a huge piece of plaster falling heavily into the empty grate.

After a time the noises entirely ceased and I was about to drop asleep, when a hoarse and despairing cry, as of some one being strangled close to my bed, rang through the panelled chamber, and brought me again to a sitting position, with all my pulses quickened to the utmost by apprehension and the vague sense of sudden alarm.

"This can no longer be borne!" I exclaimed.

Starting from bed I drew my sword, and unbolting my door issued forth into the gallery which overlooked the stable-yard.

The night, or rather the morning-air, was mild and balmy; the wind had died away, and all was calm and still. I heard the clock of the Guildhall strike the hour of two. No other sound stirred the air; and as noises at that still hour are so deceptive—though there was something in that hoarse cry which impressed me with horror—a dread of ridicule, or of being the victim of some piece of waggery, prevented me from summoning the domestics of the inn; so once more I bolted the door, put my sword at the head of the bed, and therein ensconcing myself, soon fell sound asleep.

The next day was rather far advanced when I woke up and started from bed, on instantly remembering that I must be gone without delay.

During a hasty breakfast I could not refrain from speaking to the landlord of the noises which had disturbed me so much in my chamber.

"Was the wind high or stormy last night?" I began.

"No; the weather was rather calm," said he, with his mouth full, for he was making a hearty, old-fashioned breakfast of sliced beef, and nut-brown, home-brewed ale.

"Were any persons quarrelling or fighting hereabout?"

"When?"

"Why, all night; till two in the morning at least."

"I heard not a sound—the house was perfectly quiet." This statement the waiter, ostler, and landlady hastened to corroborate.

"Then," said I, "by Jove your inn is haunted."

"Take care what you say, my good fellow," replied the landlord, becoming angry; "for lookee, my house has as good a reputation as any in the county of Surrey, so none of your tricks, soldier."

"Then the devil was in my chimney all last night, say what you will," I responded with equal, if not greater, irritation.

On hearing this the landlord's colour changed visibly. He went immediately to my room, accompanied by a servant, who soon returned making a great outcry, and stating that a man had been found wedged in the chimney, that by looking up with a lighted candle, his heels could be seen dangling some five feet or more above the mantelpiece.

On hearing these tidings, the whole

household became excited, and crowded to the apartment I had so lately quitted.

On looking up I could see, amid the obscurity of the chimney, the feet of a man, but they were beyond our reach. Workmen were soon procured; the panelling was removed; then the bricks were taken out, a breach made, and in something less than an hour, the dead body of a man was exhumed, all begrimed and covered with soot and lime.

He had evidently died of suffocation, having reached a portion of the chimney where he could neither descend further nor work his way up again, and had there miserably perished; being literally choked by the soot and lime, of which he had inhaled such quantities in his fruitless struggles and painful gaspings, that his foam-covered mouth and bloodshot eyes were quite filled with them.

His left hand was found to have been recently mutilated; his right still grasped a sharp clasp knife, which was doubtless intended for *my* behoof, as an examination proved the body to be that of the traveller who had occupied No. 6, in the upper gallery—the figure I had detected, watching in the gloom, when retiring to rest.

As some housebreaking implements were found in his pocket, the landlord averred that he had been in search of the strong-box and plate-room; but I had my own idea of his too probable errand, and thus the terrible sounds which had so long disturbed me, and that last hoarse cry of despair and death, were completely accounted for.

Fearing that I might be detained until a coroner's inquest had been held, concerning the death of this highwayman and would-be assassin, while all the inn people, guests, and servants, were full of dismay by the discovery, I saddled my grey, and set forth for my destination at a spanking pace which soon left Guildford far behind.

Before the evening gun had boomed from Southsea Castle I had reached Portsmouth, delivered my despatches and reported myself at head-quarters.

I was heartily welcomed by Charters and Kirkton, who had been sent by Colonel Preston to join Lindsay's light troop. I rejoiced at this, having sorely missed their society and companionship.

My few hours of freedom and romance —for there was something of romance in Aurora possessing my fortune, and I only her handkerchief—were now at an end, and again I was simply Basil Gauntlet the private dragoon.

CHAPTER XV.

SAIL FOR FRANCE.

By the last day of May, all the troops destined for the hostile expedition were embarked on board of the ships of war and transports. In all there were thirteen thousand fighting men, with sixty pieces of cannon, and fifty mortars.

The embarkation of our horses was an object of peculiar care, and General Elliot, with Captain Lindsay, of ours, superintended this duty in person—for on the manner in which it is performed, depends all the chance of cavalry being employed with success in the field after landing.

They were conveyed on board the various ships, after a short march of exercise, and when perfectly *cool.* On the first night after embarkation, each received a mash mixed with some nitre, and bran was supplied to every trooper, as the chief portion of his horse's daily ration.

Every day each dragoon had to wash with care the hoofs and fetlocks of his horse, and to sponge its face, eyes and nostrils with cold water. We had ample wind sails rigged up for air, and spare slings and bands all ready in case of illness or accident, but, fortunately, neither occurred among the nags of our troop at least.

At daybreak, on the first of June, a gun from the commodore gave the signal *for sea;* and in less than ten minutes every vessel had her anchor apeak or atrip, and her head sails filled, and soon after, with nine hearty cheers, the whole armament, consisting of twenty-four ships of war, and one hundred and forty transports, cutters and tenders, stood out into the channel, and a glorious sight they presented.

The *Essex*, a sixty-four gun-ship, commanded by our commodore, the Honourable Richard (afterwards Earl) Howe, led the van, and closely in her wake followed the *Brilliant* of thirty-six guns, commanded by Captain Hyde Parker, who was afterwards knighted for his services off the coast of America.

As the *Essex* bore across Sandown Bay, I have been told that the French deserter, Theophile Damien, assisted with his own hands to steer the ship, as if in token of the good service he meant to perform for us in future.

There was a pretty stiff breeze on this morning, and I had a dread of sea sickness, as the vessel rolled heavily, her main-deck being encumbered by stores; but the novelty of the scene and of the situation, together with the activity of the seamen, as they swarmed up aloft and lay out upon the yards, occupied all my attention for a time; and to our tars of after years, the Jacks of Anson and of Howe, in their little low cocked hats, Dutch-cut pea-jackets, petticoat trousers, and brass-buckled shoes, would present a very unusual spectacle. Certainly their costume was scarcely fitted for sending down the topgallant yards, or lying out on the man-rope to close-reef topsails in a gale of wind; but they were true tars, nevertheless.

Ere long the breeze, which had favoured us so much that the shores of England had lessened astern, veered somewhat ahead; the weather became stormy and wet, and I was glad to keep below, and share the stall of my horse. While Kirkton, Charters, and others, who had been frequently at sea before, sat out upon the booms to leeward, and smoked to fill up the time.

In their mirth and cheerfulness, they formed a contrast to the unfortunate seasick troopers, who were all huddled away in groups, seeking shelter under the lee of anything that offered itself, and who remained there in discomfort and misery, till the drum beat for all but the watch to go below and turn in.

Next day I came on deck about dawn, and joined Charters, who was one of the morning watch, and here I may mention, that when on boardship, troops are divided into three watches, and must take their share of all deck duty with the seamen. A subaltern officer has charge of each watch, and there are also, when the numbers embarked will permit it, a captain and subaltern of the day.

"Gauntlet, my lad, you look pale," said Charters, as he trod to and fro to keep himself warm; for though the month was June, the air upon the morning sea was cold, and the chill spray came flying in showers over the weather cat-heads, as the *Brilliant* sped upon her course, like all the fleet which covered the open channel, close hauled; "the morning watch is a devilish cold one, and we have no chance here of getting a hair of the dog—eh?" added my friend, laughing.

"What land is that?" I asked, with chattering teeth, while clutching the rigging with one hand, and pointing southward with the other.

"The land of France—that is Cape La Hogue," replied Charters.

"Ay," growled an old quartermaster; "yonder is the fort, with the flag flying."

The old tar's eyes must have been better than mine, which could discern neither fort nor flag; but I muffled my trooper's cloak about me, and set myself to watch the hostile shore.

The outline of the land looked dim and low, and like a dark cloud, as it rose from the grey morning sea, which was all of a dusky tint and flecked with masses of foam. The whole aspect of the fleet was gloomy and cheerless now; the decks and canvass were wet and dripping with the rain of the past night, and with the spray of the waves, for there was a heavy sea running in the channel; but anon the sun began to rise through successive bars or streaks of purple and saffron cloud; then the long lines of waves rolled after each other glittering in light. The canvass aloft became whiter; the hulls of the vessels shone and became instinct with life, as the red port lids were triced up, the snowy hammocks placed in their nettings, and the scarlet coats crowded on the decks; drums and bugles were heard from time to time, warnings for parade, orders or messing, as the swift fleet flew on at the rate of eight knots per hour, and now and then, by a signal from the commodore, the best sailers were ordered to cast a tow-line to the more slow, especially our deeply laden storeships.

On the evening of the 3rd of June we came to anchor, between Sark and Jersey, for what reason I know not. In the night we had a hurricane; one transport lost a mast, another lost her bowsprit, and a third, crowded with foot soldiers, was totally lost by running foul of a sunken rock. The boats of the *Brilliant* were piped away with great celerity, and all the troops were saved before the wreck went to pieces; but I shall never forget that horrible night—the darkness of the atmosphere, the bellowing of the wind and the roaring of the sea, while the frigate leaped, plunged and strained on her cables, like a restive horse; and then, amid all this, the danger and excitement caused by the sinking of the transport amid the obscurity of that stormy midnight sea, and the loss of life that might have ensued but for the skill and bravery of our seamen.

Jersey is so surrounded by reefs of sunken rock, that it was a miracle no more of our armament perished on this occasion.

On the morning of the 5th, the commodore signalled to weigh anchor and pursue our course.

The whole fleet ran with a fair breeze

along the coast of Normandy, and so close were we in shore, that the houses, farms, and even the inhabitants could be seen distinctly without the aid of glasses. At one place we saw a column of French Infantry on the march, with all their bayonets glittering in the sunshine; at another, where the land opened near Sainte Soule, a regiment of dragoons riding at full gallop in the direction we were pursuing.

"Tom, we shall be under fire to-morrow," said Charters, thoughtfully, as he knocked the ashes from his pipe into the palm of his left hand and scattered them to leeward.

"All the better," replied Kirkton, "the see-saw of home service has sickened me."

"And me too," added I, "and I long for some keen excitement."

"Excitement," replied Charters, "then

you are likely to have it with a vengeance, my boy! Think of thirteen thousand men invading France!"

By two o'clock p.m. we came to anchor in Cancalle Bay, on the coast of Brittany, nine miles eastward of St. Malo. The *Brilliant* lay not far from the famous rock of Cancalle, so celebrated for its oysters, the fishing of which forms one of the chief sources of local wealth.

Commodore Howe, it would appear, had now questioned narrowly the two French deserters, Theophile Damien and Benoît Bossoit, whom I had been the humble means of introducing to his notice, and discovering that they were profoundly ignorant of the whole locality, he began to suspect both their veracity and intentions, and therefore ordered them to be made close prisoners, while, accompanied by the Duke of Marlborough, Colonel

Watson our quarter-master-general, and Thierry the pilot, he went in the *Grace*, an armed cutter, to reconnoitre the Bay.

The information of two pretended deserters, as to the position and strength of batteries, and so forth, having proved perfectly erroneous, on his return the commodore ordered the Frenchmen to be searched; and then, on papers detailing the number and object of our armament being found upon them both, he forthwith ordered them to be put to death in the most summary manner.

Posted as sentinel on the poop of the *Brilliant*, I was in ignorance of all this, and was treading to and fro carbine in hand, with my eyes fixed on the rough and wooded shore of Brittany, when Captain Lindsay came on deck, harnessed in full regimentals with sword and gorget on.

"Well, Gauntlet," said he, "your two

Frenchmen have, unfortunately, proved to be impostors and spies, after all."

"Spies!" I reiterated, with some dismay.

"Yes; of the most dangerous kind."

"And what is to be done with them, sir?"

"That which the laws of war direct—ah! look yonder!"

He pointed to the *Essex*, the ship of the commodore, and a thrill of horror ran through me, on beholding two human forms run up simultaneously by the neck, to the arms of the foreyard, where they dangled for a minute in mid-air; but they were *not* meant to be hanged, as each had a cold thirty-two pound shot at his heels.

This must have been a pleasant spectacle for Thierry the pilot, who was also a Frenchman, and consequently a traitor.

A gun was fired from the bow of the *Essex;* solemnly the echoes of the sea and shore replied, and ere the last had died away, both culprits had vanished under the waves, whose ripples closed over them and left no trace behind. Then, as the pale and fierce dark face of Damien came in memory before me, I turned to my leader and said—

"Captain Lindsay, the fate of Damien forms a terrible sequel to the story of his brother."

"That story was falsehood—all," replied the captain; "he was no relation whatever of the famous would-be regicide, who was a peasant of Artois. The name of the spy was Theophile Hautois, not Damiens, and he never was a privateersman, nor served under Thurot, but was a forester of Brittany, and, as some suppose, a robber among the Menez Mountains. His whole narrative, so far as he was concerned, proves an artful forgery, and, like his companion, he was a fully accredited spy of the French authorities, employed to obtain information which his lips can never render them now."

The boom of a second cannon now pealed across the Bay.

"The commodore has fired another gun and hoisted a signal," said an officer close by.

The signal midshipman raised his telescope to the bunting which we saw fluttering at the mainmast-head of the *Essex*.

"What is it now—what says the order?" asked several, with the impatience and curiosity natural enough at such a time.

"All ships having flat-bottomed boats and landing-stages, *to hoist them out!*"

replied the middy, with a kindling eye.

"Bravo," added Captain Lindsay; "that seems like work! Ere long we shall have to look to our spurleathers and spatterdashes."

CHAPTER XVI.

THE LANDING AT CANCALLE.

It was very singular that though our armament had been visible off the coasts of Normandy and Brittany for four days, no preparations were made anywhere to oppose us. A strong French fleet lay in the harbour of Brest, but was there blocked up by the squadrons of Lord Anson and Sir E. Hawke, so it might as well have been in the Yellow Sea.

Just as the commodore's last signal concerning the boats was hoisted, two troops of French cavalry, and a regiment of infantry, appeared on the heights above the Bay of Cancalle, where we saw their appointments and weapons glittering; but after a time they fell back and disappeared inland.

The flat-bottomed boats were soon launched, and the grenadier companies of eleven regiments rendezvoused on board of them, around the *Essex*, the head-quarter ship.

The commodore now shifted his broad pennant on board the *Success*, a frigate of twenty-two guns, which got under weigh, and stood close inshore to silence a battery of only *three* guns, which had begun to fire across the bay.

These were the first hostile shots I had heard; and I must own that they caused my pulses to quicken, and created an undefined anxiety in my heart; yet I had already stood fire, when so narrowly escaping Abraham Clod's gun on the roof of old Wylie's stable, and that adventure made me smile when I thought of it then.

Those three cannons—two 24's and one 12-pounder—were all we had as yet to oppose, and they were in position at the landing-place of the fisher-town or village of Cancalle, which consisted of a group of picturesque little houses, situated at the base of a green hill that overhangs the sea.

The French cannoniers who handled them were brave fellows, for they killed several men on board the *Success*, nor were they silenced, and the beach swept of the inhabitants, till the commodore's ship, together with the *Rose*, *Flamborough*, and *Diligence*, opened their broadsides to the land, and filled the whole bay with smoke, making every rock and mountain echo to the reverberations of a cannonade that lasted till seven in the evening, for we had a dread of masked batteries among the shrubberies and hedgerows near the shore.

Under cover of this fire, the flat-bottomed boats, with three battalions of the Guards, and eleven grenadier companies of the Line, commanded by Lord George Sackville (son of Lionel, Duke of Dorset) and General Dury, rowed inwards, and landed on the beach in safety.

Those ships which contained the cavalry and artillery were now ordered to draw closer inshore. Our horses were slung over into the flat-bottomed boats alongside —each trooper, fully accoutred, standing in the wooden stall by his charger's head. It was about eleven at night before the light troop of the Greys, in four large flat barges, put off for the harbour, towards which we were slowly towed by the boats of the *Brilliant*.

The night was a lovely one. High

sailed the moon in heaven, with clouds of fleecy whiteness flying past her silver disc. The beach and the blue sea were light as if at noonday, and on the far expanse of yellow sand, in that secluded cove, where the aged oak and lime trees spread their summer foliage on the ripples—sand so soft, so smooth and golden that one could only think of nymphs or fairies disporting in fantastic dances there—we were disembarking Horse, Foot, and Artillery, with loaded arms and lighted matches, in all the grim array of war.

Slowly the huge boats, with their freight of Cavalry crept inshore. Streaming from behind the dark mountains, the moonlight fell in long and tremulous lines of silver sheen, in which our weapons and the trappings of man and horse glittered gaily, and the whole scene was picturesque and impressive.

Each after each, the lights that whilome twinkled in the little town went out, as we supposed the people were taking to flight, and soon obscurity veiled it all, save where one or two tapers seemed to indicate a sick room, or a student's vigil—if, indeed, at such a time, one could be philosopher enough to study.

Our Foot, already formed in quarter distance columns, after their colours were uncased, their flints and priming inspected, were silent and still; thus, save the occasional neigh of our horses, as they snuffed the land, with necks outstretched and nostrils quivering, there was no sound along the bay, but the murmur of the rising tide, when it chafed on the steep Rock of Cancalle.

Beside me stood Jack Charters, tall, erect, and soldier like. One hand grasped his horse's bridle, the other rested in the steel basket hilt of his long broad sword. With a keen, bright eye, and a proud smile on his lip, he was looking at the shore, where—like myself—he hoped to regain by bravery and courage the position he had lost by his own youthful folly and the injustice of others.

At last we were alongside the rough pier of Cancalle, and some of Kingsley's Grenadiers, who were ordered to assist in getting the Cavalry and Artillery disembarked, ran the landing stages on board for our horses. The first of ours, on *terra firma*, mounted, and sword in hand, was our gallant leader, Captain Frank Lindsay.

"Quick, my lads—get on shore and join the captain," said Charters, who, although a corporal now, could not forget the authority he had once wielded; "he is a man to stand by, for true it is that a good officer to lead makes a good soldier to follow."

"Ay, ay," added Kirkton, as he, too, leaped joyously into his saddle, and made his horse curvet, while he sung:—

"'Tis he, you, or I,
Cold, hot, wet, or dry,
We're always bound to *follow*, boys,
And scorn to fly."

"Fall in, my lads—fall in as you come ashore—and take up your dressing by the standard," cried Captain Lindsay.

A seaman, a good-natured fellow, was assisting me with my horse across the landing stage, when there was a whizzing sound, and a shot that came, no one knew from where, shattered his right elbow. He uttered a groan, and would have fallen between the boat and pier, had not Sergeant Duff, of the Greys, caught him in his arms.

"Never mind, mates," said he, cheerfully; "tie up the stump, some one—I'm in for a pension at Chatham Chest, boys!"

I remember that my first emotion was a selfish thankfulness that the shot had not struck *me*.

So strong was the ground by nature, in the neighbourhood of our landing, that two thousand determined men might have cut to pieces ten times their number from behind the thick hedgerows, the houses and the rocks; yet we encountered not the slightest opposition, save from the little battery already mentioned.

By the noon of the 6th of July, everything belonging to our small army—its whole material of war—was ashore, and we encamped on an eminence which was crowned by a picturesque old windmill.

It overlooked Cancalle, from whence

the people—all hard-featured, ungainly, and squalid-looking Bretons—had now entirely fled, leaving their houses to the mercy of our soldiers and sailors, who pillaged them of everything they could find or destroy.

On the night of the 6th, with twenty other Scots Greys, I was detailed for out-picket; and under a Captain Wilmot Brook, of the 11th Light Dragoons, with twenty men of that regiment, all supplied with one meal of cooked food for ourselves and forage for our horses, we rode two miles to the front, on the road that leads from Cancalle to St. Malo. There the captain chose a position for his picket, and threw out a line of videttes, whose orders were to keep a sharp look-out, on peril of their lives; to fire their carbines on the approach of any armed party, but to permit all persons who came singly, bearing provisions for sale, to pass to their rear, without exacting a fee for their passage—to observe well the country in their front, and to communicate whatever they saw that seemed hostile or suspicious, by signal or otherwise, to each other, and at once to the officer in command of the outpost.

These orders were rhymed rapidly over to me about nightfall, and I was left for a two hours' vigil, in a gloomy hollow way between two hills, about eight hundred yards in front of the mainbody of the picket. This was my *first* responsible duty, and it so nearly ended in bringing me to a disgraceful and violent death, that the narration of that night's adventure deserves a chapter to itself.

CHAPTER XVII.

THE VIDETTE.

To a young soldier few duties or situations are more trying than the post of advanced sentinel by night, in a strange place and foreign country, in time of war and danger —all the more so, perhaps, if the said soldier be a Scotsman, imbued with some of those superstitions, which few of his countrymen are without.

"Keep your ears and eyes open, young man," said Captain Brook as he left me. "Remember that you are not now a sentry at the gate of a home-barrack, which no one thinks of attacking, but that you are an advanced vidette, on whose vigilance and acuteness depend the safety of the picket, the honour of the army, and hence, perhaps, of the nation itself."

"Does he deem me stupid, or what?" thought I, with some pique, as he rode off, accompanied by Sergeant Duff of ours, and I was left alone—alone to my own reflections.

The moon which shone so brightly last night was now hidden by masses of cloud, yet a few stray beams lighted the landscape at a distance. In the immediate foreground, and around me, all was sunk in darkness and obscurity; but after my eyes became accustomed to the gloom, I could make out the form of the two rugged eminences or hills which overhung my post, and the pathway that wound from thence into the defile between them.

Beyond that defile I could see the

distant country, lighted at times, as I have said, by the fitful gleams of the moon.

All was still and I heard only the champing of my horse upon his powerful military bit, as I sat with the butt of my carbine planted on my right thigh, gazing steadily at the darkened pass in my front.

The time passed slowly.

Twice I threw the reins across my left arm, and twice cocked and levelled my carbine, for on each occasion figures seemed to enter the pass, some on horseback and others on foot; but the next moment showed them to be only fashioned by my overheated fancy, out of the long weeds and nettles that waved to and fro on the night wind between me and the faint moonlight beyond.

On each of these occasions I made a narrow escape; to have fired my carbine would have drawn the whole line of pickets to the front, and brought the entire army under arms; but then to give a *false* alarm is a crime to be punished, though not quite so severely as to omit an alarm when necessary; so my position was sufficiently perplexing.

Silence, night, and loneliness induced reverie, and from the present and from the future, memory carried me back to the past—that period which possessed so little that was bright for me.

But a few months before, how little could I have imagined, or anticipated, that I should become a soldier and be situated as I was then—a lonely sentinel amid the mountains of Brittany! I thought with some growing repugnance of war, its cruelties and stern necessities—the precipitate execution of the two unfortunate spies, and the mangled corpses of the slain seamen, whom I had seen flung like lumber from the lower deck ports of the *Success*, after she engaged the battery in the Bay of Cancalle, and a shudder came over me, for I was young to such work as this.

I thought of the green mountains of my native land—that lovely Borderland, and its chain of hills that rise from sea to sea, between the sister kingdoms, with their fertile glens where herd and hirsel grazed in peace; where the brown eagle had his eyry in the grey rocks, and the black raven soared high in mid-air or came swooping down when the silvery salmon, or the spotted trout leaped up from the plashing linn—the land where every cairn and wood, tower and tree, had some wild or warlike legend of the past.

Old Netherwood, too, with the lazy rooks that cawed among its oaks, or roosted on the creaking vanes of its time-worn turrets. Then I turned away my thoughts in anger to the secluded Border village, where I had been so long a drudge, yea a very slave; but with the memory of old Nathan's inky desk, came a pleasant vision of the pretty little Ruth—Ruth whom I had well-nigh forgotten.

Was Ruth unmarried still? Did she ever think of me? I could almost laugh at my first love already, for to this heresy will the mind come at times, and in barracks I had reached it already.

And then Aurora—my gay and dashing cousin Aurora—the fair usurper of all that was mine, did she ever think of me, and our race on Banstead Downs? And so, soaring away into the realms of fancy, I forgot all about the pass in my front and the picket in my rear, till the sudden and confused explosion of some twenty carbines about a hundred yards distant, on my right, all flashing redly through the darkness, gave me a start, a shock, as if struck by lightning; and before I had time to think or act, there came the rush of many hoofs, and then a party of French Hussars, all fleetly mounted, swept past me from the *rear*, and fled towards the pass, pursued by our picket, which was led by Captain Brook in person! My horse reared wildly as they all passed me, and for about ten minutes I remained irresolute and ignorant what to do, until the captain with the main body of the picket all safe and untouched, but breathless and highly excited, came back at a hand gallop.

Now, for the first time I discovered that during my luckless reverie a party of French light horse, commanded, it afterwards appeared, by the Chevalier de

Boisguiller, an officer of dashing bravery, had crept past me at the distance of fifty yards or so, and unmolested and unchallenged, had actually ridden so close to Brook's picket, that they were first discovered by their sabres glittering in the light of the watchfire, near which the captain was seated.

Brook's face was crimson, and his voice hoarse with rage and passion when he accosted me, and in a minute more I found myself dismounted, disarmed, and standing a prisoner before him, a dragoon being on each side of me with his carbine loaded.

The captain was a handsome and soldierlike man, somewhere about forty-five years of age, and the blue uniform of the 11th Light Dragoons, faced and lapelled with buff to the waist, and richly laced with gold, became him well. His features, though naturally of a grave and mild cast, were now stern, and his eyes sparkled with anger. I could see all this by the light of a torch, held by one of the 11th, and I could perceive also that my comrades of the Greys regarded me with aught but pleasant faces, as I had involved the honour of the corps by my negligence.

"So—so—s'death, you are a fine fellow to act as a vidette!" began the captain, with scorn and wrath in his tone; "thanks to you, we have had an alert with a vengeance! You are now aware, that while asleep you have permitted a body of the enemy's cavalry to pass your post—a body which, if strong enough, would have cut this picket to pieces."

"Under favour, sir, I was not asleep," said I, firmly.

"Zounds, sirrah, it matters little! But do you know what the 'Articles of

War' say concerning conduct such as yours?"

I was silent.

"Shall I tell you?" asked the captain, earnestly, and in a lower tone.

"If you please."

"They state that any officer or soldier who shall shamefully abandon any fortress, *post or guard*, committed to his charge, or who shall be found sleeping on his post, whether upon the land or the sea, shall suffer DEATH, or such other punishment as a court martial may award."

I was so completely stunned by all this as to be incapable of speech; but Duff of ours, a kind and grey-haired old sergeant, said—

"Captain Brook, the lad is a good lad, and a steady one; we have few better in the Greys—"

"Then I am very sorry for the Greys!"

"I do hope, sir," continued the sergeant, "that his life, at least, may not be forfeited?"

"My life!" I exclaimed, mechanically.

"Yes, that may be forfeited, and I disgraced!" said Captain Brook, bitterly. "I have commanded many a post, but never one that was surprised before. To-morrow I shall hand you over to the guard of the provost marshal. What is your name, fellow?"

"Basil Gauntlet."

On hearing this, he started and became so visibly affected, that the soldiers of the picket who crowded round us holding their horses by the bridle, glanced at each other with inquiry and surprise. Brook surveyed me keenly for a moment, and then a sorrowful frown seemed to deepen on his features.

"Was your father ever in the service?" he asked, abruptly.

"He was an officer of Granby's Dragoons."

Then a malignant light sparkled in the eyes of Captain Brook, and he struck his spurred heel into the turf.

"Was my father your friend?" I asked, with hesitation.

"Friend!" he reiterated, bitterly; "no—no—not my friend. But your mother, what of her?" he added, in an altered voice.

"She is in her grave," I replied, with faltering accent; "else, perhaps, I had not stood before you thus to-night, a private soldier and a prisoner."

After a pause—

"My God!" said Brook, in a low voice, as he took off his helmet and passed a hand across his flushed brow. Then seeming to recollect himself, he said, "Fall back, sergeant; and fall back, men —picket your horses, and lie down if you please till daybreak, when the outpickets are called in. Leave the prisoner with me. Gauntlet," he continued, after we were somewhat alone, "step with me this way. I shall do all in my power to serve you, and to be your friend."

"Sir, you astonish me," I exclaimed; "how am I so fortunate?"

"I will tell you a secret, boy—a secret long buried in my heart," he continued, in a voice that grew soft and kind; "your father and I were rivals—rivals for the love of the same girl, long, long years ago; but he was the successful wooer—I the discarded one! She was your mother, boy, and now, for her sacred memory, and the memory, too, of that early love, which brightened for a time the first days of my soldiering, I will save you, my poor lad, if I can. Nay more, I have some interest at head-quarters, and will serve you as if you had been my own son, and this will I do for *her* sake."

The voice of Captain Brook trembled, and I bowed low, for I could not speak.

"You know what the rules of the service prescribe," he resumed, "in such a case as yours?"

"You have already told me, sir."

"Death!"

"Yes."

"Yet, you shall not die, and your future promotion shall be my peculiar care. Comrades," cried he, to the men of the picket, "in Basil Gauntlet I have discovered the son of an early and dear friend. He is but a young soldier—a mere boy, and I would save him if I can."

"You may command us, sir," said Sergeant Duff.

"We will do anything for you, Captain Brook," added the men of the 11th, with enthusiasm.

"I do not mean to report his dereliction of duty—so give me your words that *you* will be silent in the matter."

"We swear it, sir!" they exclaimed, with energy, and that honest pledge was never broken.

"Now, Basil Gauntlet," said Captain Brook, as he gave me back my sword, and grasped my hand, while speaking rapidly and energetically; "you, doubtless, have your father's courage and spirit of honour. These are hereditary, and old Sir Basil could not *will them away* as he did the acres of Netherwood, the family pictures, and the silver spoons. Be a man, and a brave one, as your father was—I knew him well and hated him—God rest him now, for all that. To-morrow, I shall see that you are taken out of the ranks; for, to-night, I can but share with you the contents of my canteen."

An aide-de-camp now came galloping from Cancalle to inquire the meaning of the firing. Some explanation, I know not what, was made, and so ended this remarkable episode, which had a gloomy sequel on the morrow, when all the bright future, which the sudden friendship of Captain Brook had opened to me, was rapidly overcast.

About noon the poor man was killed by a shot from a French sharpshooter, as we were advancing through a thick wood. Dr. Lancelot Probe of ours was speedily at hand, but my new friend was gone for ever, and I was one of those who assisted to wrap his remains in a horse rug, and to inter them by the wayside, as we marched towards St. Malo.

CHAPTER XVIII.

HALT AT ST. SERVAND.

During the 7th of June the whole force (save one regiment, which was left at Cancalle to cover our re-embarkation, if necessary) marched towards St. Malo, through a rough and woody country. A dense mist from the ocean enveloped the scenery for some miles inland, and through this we were advancing when Captain Brook was killed. The soil seemed barren, with black sheep grazing among the rocks and boulders; old and ruinous bridges lay across deep swamps and rugged watercourses, that rushed towards the sea. Without molestation we passed several quaint, old manor houses, girdled by weedy fosses and moss-grown oaks—and some whose embattled *porte cocher* and grated casements opened to long and shady avenues of sycamore trees.

Ere long, we came to more open parts of the country, covered with pink heath and spotted with yellow flowers; in others, with fields, snow white with the bloom of buckwheat. In these flat places rose here and there, exactly as in Scotland, great battle stones of the Druids or the Celtic Bretons, that stood grim, grey, erect, solemn and silent; and so a march of nine miles through scenery such as this brought us in sight of St. Malo.

The men of our troop were so much occupied in scouring the district through which the infantry advanced, covering both flanks, reconnoitring and so forth, that it was not until sunset when our small army encamped at the village of St. Servand, two miles from St. Malo, that I had an opportunity of relating to my two chief friends, Tom Kirkton and Jack Charters, the strange adventure of the preceding night.

They listened to me with astonishment, as we sat by the foot of a large tree under which our horses were stabled (if I may use such a term), and where we were regaling ourselves with ration biscuits and the contents of a gallon keg of French wine, of which Charters had become proprietor on the march.

Around us the whole force, horse, foot, and artillery, were busy cooking or preparing for the bivouac of the night. Countless little fires, lighted beside trees, hedges, and low walls, glared and reddened in the evening wind, and when the dusk set in, they shed a wavering gleam on the piles of arms that stood in long ranks, on the white bell-tents and the red-coated groups that loitered near. The whole scene was picturesque, lively, and striking, and in the distance lay the town and fortress of St. Malo, quaint and worn by time and the misty storms that came from the open sea.

Its harbour is one of the best seaports in France, but is extremely difficult of access. The town is small, gloomy, and dull, but populous and wealthy, and crowns a rock which the sea encompasses twice daily—thus St. Malo is alternately insular and peninsular, as the tide ebbs, flows, and churns in foam against its fetid rocks, whereon the russet-brown seaweed rots in the sunshine; and far around it lies a barrier of sharp white reefs, the foe of many a ship ere beacons were invented.

It was guarded by a strong castle, flanked by great towers, on the battlements of which the last light of the setting sun yet lingered with a fiery gleam. The town had usually a good garrison; but His Grace the Duke of Marlborough had now learned that there were not quite five hundred troops in the whole of this neglected province of Brittany, which, though forming a portion of the kingdom of France, had long been under its hereditary dukes, and was now governed by a States General, with provincial privileges of its own.*

For ages so separate had its interests been from those of France, that James III. of Scotland was requested by Charles VIII. to send thither a body of troops to capture and annex Brittany to his northern kingdom; but the Scottish parliament declined

* It continued so until the Revolution in 1792.

to sanction the subjugation of a free people; so this strange scheme was abandoned.

A strong wall surrounded St. Malo, and every night twelve dogs of great size and ferocity were led round it by a soldier of the city watch, that their barking might give notice if brigands or an enemy approached.

The last ray of sunlight soon faded upward from the cathedral spire of St. Vincent, and the shades of twilight were already casting into obscurity the rocky basement of the whole city and its weedy reefs amid the chafing sea, when in a lonely part of our camp by St. Servand my two comrades and I reclined on the turf beside our accoutred horses, and drank the contents of the wine-keg, using one horn—for we possessed but one—fraternally by turns.

"It is very true," continued Charters, with reference to my adventure of the preceding night; "egad, friend Gauntlet, you had a narrow escape! In other hands—particularly those of old Preston—you had assuredly been brought to the drum-head and had a volley of ten carbines for dereliction of duty. To fall asleep on one's post before an enemy——"

"But I was *not* asleep," I persisted.

"Well, well; but to let the enemy pass you——"

"I was thinking of other times, Jack."

"Very likely," said Kirkton; "on such a lonely duty, and at such a time, by night, I have too often found the thoughts of other times, and images of those I have loved or lost, who are dead, or far, far away, all come unbidden before me."

"It is unwise to look back regretfully—for the past can never come again. Oh, never more!" continued Charters, sadly, as he thought of some cherished episode of his own life; "so the wiser and the manlier way is to improve the *present* (pass the keg, Tom), and look boldly at the future."

"You are right, Jack," said I, as this military philosopher proceeded to light his pipe and groom his horse, which he carefully covered with his cloak; "but I fear it will be long before I can school myself into your cool way of taking things. I have seen but little of the world, Jack, and have only learned to enjoy life since embracing the profession which sets no value upon it."

"Time and travel will improve your views, my boy; and 'all travel,' says Dr. Johnson, 'has its advantages; if it lead a man to a better country, he learns to improve his own; if to a worse, to enjoy it.' I have travelled much in my time—steady, old horse, steady!—and as I did so with sundry rounds of ball cartridge at my back, I have learned much that Dr. Johnson never thought of."

"In what way, Jack—to handle a dice-box and make love to the barmaids?" asked Tom.

"I have learned more than that," retorted Charters, somewhat coldly; "travel taught me to be charitable; for one finds good people everywhere, abroad as well as at home, for as it takes a great many men to make an army, so many people are required to make a nation."

"Bah!" shouted Tom Kirkton, who was in his shirt-sleeves and attending to our cooking; "we have had enough of musty moralising. This is like one of old father's sermons, poor man! and a sermon sounds oddly in your mouth, Jack. Here is a rasher of bacon, broiled on a ramrod and done to a turn. Come here while it is hot and savoury, for we may say with the fool in the Scripture, 'Let us eat and drink, for to-morrow we die.'"

"Boot and saddle! To horse, you fellows there!" cried the loud and authoritative voice of a staff officer as a strange sequel to Tom's ominous speech. He proved to be General Elliot, who was passing through our bivouac at a hand gallop, accompanied by his aide-de-camp, both plumed and aiguiletted. "To horse—the Light Dragoons!"

"Fall in—the Scots Greys!" added Captain Lindsay, coming up at a trot; "we are ordered to the front."

So Tom's dainty rasher was eaten in a trice; the last of Charters's wine was drained, the keg tossed into the nearest watch fire, we sprang on our horses, and at the first ruffle on the kettle-drum, formed line on the left of our standard.

CHAPTER XIX.

THE SACK OF ST. SOLIDORE.

Like all who are so subordinate in rank, we fell in and formed, in total ignorance of where we were going, or what we were to do; who we were to attack, or by whom we might be attacked; and, perhaps, not caring much about the matter, provided we were to do something.

In the dusk the roll was called; the troop "proved" and formed in column with the other light troops under Elliot, the future "Cock of the Rock." We loaded our carbines and pistols, and then the order was given—

"Threes right—forward—trot!" and away we went.

Though we had been imbibing only French wine, we three comrades were not in a very reputable condition; but, fortunately, this could not be perceived in the twilight; though Charters was unusually lively, and my skill was frequently tested, as I was generally the flanker of a squadron, being completely master of my horse.

In the leading section of three, there was a gigantic trooper before us, named Hob Elliot.

"By Jove, Hob, what a noble pair of shoulders you have!" said Charters, as we trotted on; "what a mark your back will be for our friends the French!"

"If they ever *see* it," growled the Borderer, for he was a Liddesdale man.

"Bravo, Gauntlet," hiccupped Charters, then turning to me; "head up, and thumb on the bridle—you have quite the air of a soldier!"

"I always study to *be* what I wish to seem," said I.

"So said Socrates," added Tom Kirkton, remembering his classics.

"Ugh! he quotes Socrates on the line of march."

"Well," rejoined Tom; "he was a private soldier like ourselves, and saved the life of Xenophon."

"Be silent, my lads," said Captain Lindsay; "we have work in hand that requires you to be so."

As we quitted our bivouac, I was more than ever struck with its picturesque aspect. Some regiments of infantry (among them the 8th, 20th, and 25th), which had not yet been ordered under arms, were lying around their watchfires in a green clover field. These fires could not have been less than ninety or a hundred in number, and their united glare fell redly on the sunburned faces and scarlet uniforms of the scattered groups who sat around them; on the lines of those who lay asleep with their knapsacks for pillows; on the long rows of muskets, piled with bayonets fixed, and on the silk colours, that drooped before the guarded tent of each commanding officer.

Beyond these were the dark figures of the active artillery, limbering up, tracing their horses to the field guns, and preparing for immediate service; and as fresh fuel was cast on those watchfires, and the weird light flared up anew, it brought out in strong relief objects at a greater distance; trees and rocks were visible for a time, and then, as the flame wavered and sunk, they faded into obscurity. Add to all this, that the night was intensely dark, and the atmosphere dense and sulphury.

Nor moon nor star were visible; the

wind was still, and the flames of the crackling watchfires burned steadily and high.

"Where are we going—what are we to be about?" we now inquired of each other as we rode on; and ere long, from mouth to mouth, as the staff officers, perhaps, unwisely informed those commanding troops, and these, in turn their subs, we learned that the Duke of Marlborough had, during the day, reconnoitred the harbour and suburbs of St. Malo, with the shipping and government stores, and had resolved on their destruction; so we were now to cover the advance of a body of infantry and artillery who were to perform this duty, with shot, shell, and hand grenades.

While advancing, I overheard Captain Lindsay say to Cornet Keith of ours—

"Marlborough has heard that the youngest and favourite daughter of the

Marshal de Broglie, who now commands in Germany, resides in a chateau near St. Malo; and he thinks she would prove an important capture."

"Nay—pshaw—zounds, gallantry forbid!" responded the cornet, who was carrying the standard.

"I heard him say he would give a hundred and fifty guineas for her," continued Lindsay.

"For what purpose?" asked Keith, laughing.

"To send to London as a trophy, like the brass guns we hope to take at Cherbourg."

"A sorry capture, unless the girl is beautiful."

After proceeding about half a mile, our troop was ordered to press forward to the front, while the others reined up; then, as the artillery halted, and the deep hollow rumbling of the wheels and shot-laden tumbrils ceased, we could hear the flowing tide chafing in the dark on the bluff rocks of St. Malo, and, ere long, we saw the red lights that twinkled in its streets and fortress which towered above the ocean.

Girt as it was by deep waves and lofty walls, "the city of the corsairs," as some one names it, was secure from us then; so we rode on till we reached an open space, when the order came to form line on the leading section, and then the whizz, whizz, whizzing of balls, together with the rapid flashing of carbines in front, announced that the foe was before us.

My temples throbbed; there was a wild glow in my heart, and then an emotion of terror, as a bullet struck me fairly in the centre of the breast, above my pouch belt. For an instant I thought it was through me, and breathlessly dropped my reins; then, instinctively, I placed my hand within my coat, and expecting to find it covered with blood, drew forth—what? Aurora's handkerchief. It had saved me from the ball, which pierced my coat, though half spent.

I pressed it to my parched lips in gratitude; and perfume was lingering about it still. I had scarcely replaced it and recovered my equanimity, when I heard the clear, firm voice of Captain Lindsay, as he rode to the front, with young Keith by his side, carrying the standard advanced.

"Cavalry are before us, and we must clear the way. March—trot! keep your horses well in hand—press on by leg and spur!"

We advanced, with drawn swords, the troop riding on, boot to boot, and thigh to thigh—moving like a living wall. Then rapidly followed the words—

"Gallop—*charge!*" mingling with the sharp blast of the trumpet, and totally ignorant of what was amid the darkness in our front, whether a column of cavalry, a yawning chasm, or a stone rampart, we rushed blindly and furiously on with a loud and ringing cheer.

We charged with tremendous force, and in the heat, hurry, and confusion of such a moment, performed at racing speed, I sat in my saddle and guided my horse with a combined coolness and steadiness that certainly resulted from mere instinct or force of habit, rather than reason. I felt as in a dream, till suddenly, out of the darkness in front, there came before me a line of horses' heads, with another line of human faces, and uplifted swords above them. Then there was a wild crash, as if the earth had opened, when horse and man went tumbling under us, as we swept over the enemy, cutting and treading them down.

"*Tuè! Tuè!*" cried they; "St. Malo for Brittany!" But their provincial patron availed them not.

They proved to be a mere handful of hussars, led by the Chevalier de Boisguiller, who was nearly killed by the sword of Charters; but escaped by having an iron calotte cap within his fur cap. We lost only three men in this charge; but found nine of the enemy lying dead on the ground next day.

In vain the Chevalier, an officer of the most romantic courage, endeavoured to rally his men.

"*En avant, mes camarades—Mes enfans, en avant!*" we heard him shout, while brandishing his sabre; "*Voilà—voilà, c'est la voye à l'honneur, à la gloire, à la victoire! Vive le Roi!*"

As they fled there was no pursuit, for the trumpet sounded to recal stragglers.

Then we reformed line and wheeled back, to permit the infantry and artillery to pass to the front. After this, our orders were simply to guard and patrol the approaches to St. Solidore, against which our comrades on foot commenced the most active operations.

I have no intention of detailing the whole of these, nor could I do so, perhaps, if willing; but never shall I forget the splendour of the terrible scene which ensued, when the fires of destruction spread along the suburbs of St. Solidore and St. Servand, and all around the harbour of St. Malo.

Through the dark sky we saw the shells fired by our artillery describing long arcs of light, and bursting like fiery stars or flaming comets among the rigging of the ships in the basin, or on the roofs of the stores and houses on the quay. Then the shrieks and cries of the fugitive people came towards us through the still night air, together with the incessant explosion of the hand grenades, which our grenadiers, as they advanced alongside the ships, threw point blank on their decks, and down the open hatchways.

The most deadly missiles were the *anchor balls*, fired by our artillery.

These were filled with powder, saltpetre, sulphur, resin, and turpentine, and had an iron bar, one half of which was within and the other outside the shell. The latter half was armed with a grappling-hook, which caught the rigging of the ships, or the walls or roofs of houses, as the heaviest end flew foremost, and by these chiefly the whole place was soon sheeted with flaming pyramids, amid which we saw walls crumbling and descending, and masts and yards disappearing amid mountains of sparks and burning brands, while torrents of red fire poured from every door and window round the whole circle of the harbour.

The sky was full of red clouds and sheets of red sparks; the harbour and the bay beyond were all ruddied, as if changed to port wine, and the whole air became filled with roaring flame.

High over all this towered St. Malo on its rock, and on its embattled walls, its gothic spires and storm-beaten cliffs, redly fell the glare of destruction; while at times we heard the barking of the watch dogs, and could see the gleam of arms along the ramparts, for every citizen was in harness, and from mouth to mouth went the cry.

"St. Malo for Brittany! the women to their homes, and the men to their muskets!"

But, though they knew it not, we had no idea then of assailing a place so strong by art and nature.

The naval storehouses, full of sails, ropes, tar, pitch, oil, paint and powder, blazed the whole night, exhibiting every variety of prismatic colours, but ere morning, ships, houses, and magazines were all confounded in one mass of charred and blackened ashes.

We destroyed in the docks and in the harbour thirteen vessels of war, mounting two hundred and thirty-four guns, with seventy-three merchant ships, and £800,000 worth of property, after which we retired with the loss of only twelve men, three of whom were seamen, killed by a single random shot from St. Malo.

During this wild scene, there was something singular, almost touching, in the terror of the poor birds, when the air became alive with soaring and bursting shells, with showers of shot, thick with smoke, laden with the booming of the ordnance and the ceaseless roar of the conflagration.

Crows, larks, pigeons, and sparrows seemed to become paralysed by fear; they fluttered, panted, and grovelled among the long grass and under the hedgerows, in some instances crouching and hiding themselves in little coveys close to the dead and wounded Hussars (who lay where we had charged), as if to rebuke the spirit in man that made of earth a hell!

And so thought I, when weary, wan, and pale, I retired with the troop towards our camp on the hills of Paramé.

CHAPTER XX.

AN EPISODE.

As the column of light cavalry wheeled off by sections to return to the camp and bivouac, a staff officer who was riding hurriedly past in the dark addressed me—

"Young man," said he, "do you see those lights twinkling in the hollow yonder?"

"Yes, sir; the port fires of the artillery."

"Exactly; ride with all speed to the officer commanding the brigade of guns, and say it is the order of General Elliot that he falls back at once towards the hills of Paramé."

I bowed, for the speaker was the general in person.

To execute this order, I had to ride nearly a mile to the rear, skirting the wide stretch of sand that lies between St. Malo and St. Servand. The morning was still quite dark, and the fires yet smouldered redly in the dockyards and harbour, while a heavy smoke and odour of burning loaded the air, which was very still and oppressive.

I rode towards the place, where the matches of the artillery shone brilliantly; but I had scarcely reached the flank of the brigade, when the whole force got into motion at a rapid trot, the gunners on their seats, and the drivers plying well their whips, as they wheeled off towards the hills with a tremendous noise, chains, shot, rammers, spunges, and buckets all swinging and clattering. Thus I had no occasion to deliver the anticipated orders of General Elliot; but as the artillerymen were driving with such fury, I reined up to let them pass, and followed leisurely in their rear.

Day was now beginning to break, and the summits of the hills and the spires of the city of St. Malo—in the dark ages the abode of saints, in more modern times the asylum of criminals—were brightening in the ruddy gloom; but smoke hung like a sombre pall over all the harbour below.

From time to time I could hear in the distance the hollow bay of the fierce dogs which watched the city walls, a custom that was not abolished until 1770, when one night they tore to pieces and devoured a naval officer.

The sound of water plashing by the wayside drew my horse towards it. The poor animal was thirsty after the long and weary patrol duty of the past night. The stream poured from a rock, and through a moss-green wooden duct fell into the stone basin of a wayside well, and there, while my horse drunk long and thirstily, I heard the rumble of the artillery as they passed away among the echoing mountains and I was left alone in the rear.

By the roadside near the fountain, there grew a dense thicket of mulberry trees and wild broom-bushes, from amid which—just as I was turning my horse to ride off—there rung a half-stifled cry, followed by a fierce and very unmistakeable malediction in French—for that language, and not the old Armoric, is spoken by the Bretons of Dol and St. Malo.

Supposing that some unfortunate English straggler or wounded man might be lying there at the mercy of some of the enemy, I drew a pistol from my holsters and dismounted. My horse was so well trained, that I knew he would remain where I left him, while penetrating into the thicket. The gloom of the latter was excessive, but day was breaking, and a faint light stole between the slender stems of the trees.

Two figures now appeared—those of a man and woman. Having come close upon them unobserved, I now shrunk behind a bush to watch. The woman was on her knees, and her left shoulder reclined against the root of a tree; her whole attitude indicated weariness or despair, or both together. Her hands were tied with a scarf or handkerchief, and her dark hair hung over her face so as to conceal her features entirely. Close by her, and with one hand resting against the same tree, the man stood erect, but looking down, and surveying her with some solicitude, or at least with interest. He wore a peasant's frock of blue linen, girt at the waist by a belt with a square buckle. He was armed with a small hatchet and *couteau de chasse*, and carried in his right hand a knotted cudgel.

They were quite silent; at least I heard only from time to time the half-stifled sobs of the female.

"Here is some mystery or premeditated mischief," thought I; "let me watch warily."

At last the woman said faintly—

"Release me!"

The man uttered a growling guttural laugh.

"Release me, I implore you!" she continued in a voice of great softness and pathos.

"For the hundredth time you have thus implored me, mademoiselle, and for the hundredth time I reply—never."

"My father——"

"*Tonnerre de Ciel!* don't speak to me of your father," said the man, grinding his teeth; "I was an honest woodcutter in the Black Forest of Hunandaye till he ruined me."

"Impossible! my good father is incapable of such a thing."

"Nothing is impossible to dukes and peers of France, who have the Bastille and the dungeons of their own chateaux at their command."

"But he ruined you? Alas! how?"

"By permitting his nephew — the Comte de Bourgneuf—to carry off my sister; and because I resented the act, he had my cottage demolished, my mother driven into the forest where she was devoured by wolves, and myself he chained to work like a felon on the roads and ramparts of St. Malo and the aqueducts at Dol."

"Alas! monsieur, I swear to you that my father was blameless in all this, and even were it not so, why are you so merciless to me—why make me thus your prisoner?"

"Because you are beautiful," said the fellow, with a grating laugh. "Despite these wrongs, I risked my life for France, or rather for French gold. I have been at the bottom of the sea, *pardieu!* and am now on firm land. I have been dead, and am come alive again! Ha! ha! Bourgneuf carried off my sister. I carry off you—*chacun à son gout*—(every man to his taste.")

"Ah! have mercy. See how I weep."

"Of course; weeping is a complaint that is very common among women. The count took my sister to Paris, and she was never heard of again. I shall take you to the Black Forest of Hunandaye, and never shall you be heard of either, unless your friends are rash enough to seek you in the subterranean torrent of St. Aubin du Cormier."

"This fellow is mad; but whether mad or not, I must save the poor girl at all hazards," thought I, while shaking the priming in the pan of my holster pistol.

"Have you no dread of punishment, for thus daring to molest me?" demanded the lady.

"No. Neither here nor hereafter. You shall live with me in the forest, and when tired of you——"

"I shall escape and proclaim you."

"*Pardieu!* you wont, my beauty;

because I shall kill you, and your disappearance will, like the king's ships, be set down to the score of these pestilent English, who have come hither to turn our Brittany upside down. Besides, who knows that *I* have carried you off?"

"And you will kill me—I, who never harmed you in thought, in word, or deed?" said she, with a shudder.

"Yes," he hissed through his clenched teeth.

"Oh, horror! Will no one rescue me?"

"*Oui! Sacré!* Kill you quietly and secretly, even as I killed quietly and surely the English captain of the Chevaux Légers in the wood near Cancalle yesterday."

I started on hearing this, for the assassin of poor Captain Brook of the 11th was now covered by the muzzle of *my* weapon. The speaker was a tall, rawboned fellow, whose form exhibited great strength and stature; he had a shambling gait, and a dirty visage of a very bilious complexion. His hair was black and shaggy; he had dark lack-lustre eyes and large, fierce, blubberlike lips, yellowed as his broken fangs were by coarse tobacco juice. I had somewhere before seen this hideous face, the features of which gradually came to view as the increasiug light stole gradually through the mulberry wood. How was it that this countenance, so pale and repulsive, the forehead which receded like that of a hound, the immense frontal bones, and the square jaw like that of a tiger, were in some sort not unfamiliar to me?

Though torn and in wild disorder, the dress of his prisoner, grey silk brocaded with white, evinced that she was of some rank, and her arms, which her tattered sleeves displayed almost to the shoulder, were beautiful in form and of exceeding delicacy.

"*Nombril de Belzebub!*" said he, suddenly, as he ground his teeth. "Come, come, we've had enough of this. Let us begone, lest those English wolves return."

Then the girl uttered a pitiful cry, as his huge knotty hand grasped her slender wrists.

"Kill me now!" she implored; "for mercy's sake, kill me now!"

"By no means, my beauty—you must first see the black dingles of Hunandaye. I may kiss you as often as you please, but as for killing, until I weary of you, *pardieu!* there is no chance of that."

He was now proceeding to drag her along the ground, when I rushed forward, and by a blow of my sword, felled the savage to the ground. A small cap of thick fur which he wore saved him from being cut, but not from the weight of a stunning blow.

With a dreadful Breton oath he leaped up, and with uplifted cudgel was springing on me, when on seeing my levelled pistol he paused and shrunk back, with a terrible expression of baffled rage and ferocity in his eyes.

Judge then of my astonishment on recognising in this hideous fellow the pretended French deserter, the spy, Theophile Damien or Hautois, whom I had met at Portsmouth—whom I had seen run up to the yardarm of the *Essex*, and from thence consigned to the deep with a cold thirty-two pound shot at his heels!

CHAPTER XXI.

JACQUELINE.

HAD this man a charmed life? was he a vampire, a devil, or what? thought I, as we surveyed each other, and I have no doubt he recognised me, as he had seen me thrice before. I released the lady's hands from the handkerchief which bound them, and then raised her from the ground.

Hautois again lifted his bludgeon menacingly, but lowered it when I levelled my pistol straight at his head.

"Pass on, fellow—begone," said I, "or I shall pistol you without mercy. After our work last night, you cannot imagine that taking a Frenchman's life—especially yours—is a matter of much importance to me."

"*Sangdieu!*" he growled, "what business have you to interfere here?"

"Business—rascal!"

"Yes—this woman is my wife, who wishes to run away from me."

"Oh, horror! oh, absurdity!" exclaimed the young lady, as she gathered her dark hair back from her face with her pretty hands, and shrunk close to me.

"*Sangdieu*—yes, my wife, I tell you," shouted the fellow, with a hand on the *couteau de chasse* in his girdle; but I replied—

"I have overheard enough to prove that you lie, villain; so begone at once, I say, or be punished as you deserve. Come, madam, permit me to assist you; my horse is close by, and from our camp at

Paramé you shall have a safe escort to your home."

She took my proffered hand with a very mingled or doubtful expression of face, for I was a stranger, a soldier, an enemy; but she had only a choice of evils, and knew that probably she could not fall into worse hands than those from which I took her. Then as I was leading her away, with her dark eyes fixed in terror and aversion on Hautois, she uttered a shrill cry which made me start and turn round; and I did so just in time to escape a deadly thrust aimed at my back. Indeed, the sharp blade of the *couteau de chasse* passed through my coat, grazing my left ribs, and almost severing my buff waist-belt.

Exasperated by this, I resolved to pistol the ruffian at once, and shot him through the jaws. On this, he fell on his face, wallowing in blood, and rolled among the long grass, with his hands pressed upon the wound in each cheek. The wretch was only wounded, however, not killed. The girl whom I had rescued was fainting with terror at this scene, so I hurried her off to where my horse still stood quietly by the wayside well.

Day had completely broken now, and I could perceive that my fair companion was undoubtedly a young lady of great beauty and polished manners. She was ghastly pale, doubtless with the terrors of the past night, and the extreme darkness of her hair and eyes served but to increase, by contrast, the pallor of her complexion. Her hands, which were without gloves, proved her high breeding and delicate nurture, by their charming form and whiteness. The morning air was chill and damp, for the dews of night yet gemmed every leaf and blade of grass; and she shuddered with cold or fear, for she was without a head-dress, and her general attire was rather thin and scanty.

"You will permit me," said I, taking the cloak from my saddle and wrapping it round her; "and now say, to where can I escort you?"

"Not to the British camp, if possible, I pray you," she replied, while beginning to weep freely.

"I dare not be absent long," said I; "my duty leads me there, and by straggling, or loitering here——"

"True—true, *ah, mon Dieu!* how selfish of me! you risk your life, perhaps, at the hands of our exasperated peasantry."

"Madam, I risk my life daily for a trooper's pay," said I, smiling: "so freely may I peril it for one so—so lovely as you."

She coloured at this reply, and drew back, on which I added, with a low bow, while my cheek reddened also—

"Pardon me—I forget myself."

"This is not the bearing or the language of an English private soldier," said she, approaching me again, placing her pretty hand upon my arm, and looking pleadingly in my face.

"Madam, though but a *simple soldat—un Ecossais Gris*, I am a gentleman, and have never done aught to disgrace my name."

"Then you will protect me, sir, will you not?"

"As I have already done, at the peril of my life."

"And *not* take me to the camp?"

"Not if safer shelter can be found."

"Even if I tell you who I am?" she continued, with a proud smile.

"Yes; but who——"

"I am the daughter of a French soldier."

"Thus you have an additional claim on my honour, madam."

"Mademoiselle—I am unmarried," she urged, with the faintest approach to coquetry in her dark eyes.

"And the daughter of a soldier, say you?"

"Le Maréchal Duc de Broglie."

"Who now commands in Germany?" I continued, with growing interest.

"The same, monsieur."

The scrap of conversation I had overheard between Captain Lindsay and Cornet Keith, during the night march, now flashed upon my memory.

"Pray tell no one else who you are," said I, hurriedly, while looking around me.

"*Pourquoi, monsieur?*" she asked, with almost hauteur.

"Because I heard an officer of rank say, that he would give a hundred and fifty English guineas to have you taken prisoner, and sent to London as a trophy."

She trembled and shrunk back on hearing this, lifting up her white hands deprecatingly.

"Oh be not alarmed, Mademoiselle de Broglie," said I, "for I would rather die than betray you."

"And how much may this reward be in French money?"

"About two thousand livres."

"Two thousand livres," she exclaimed, with a haughty laugh and a flashing eye; "they hold me cheap, indeed, who offer this!"

"Pardon me, mademoiselle," said I,

anxiously, "but I have no time to lose in having you conveyed to a place of safety. If absent from morning roll call, my punishment will not be slight. The peasantry have all fled inland——"

"But surely in some farmhouse or cottage I may find shelter."

"How comes it to pass the ruffian Hautois is still alive?" I asked, as we walked along the road with the bridle of my horse over my arm. "He was cast into the sea from the yard-arm of our commodore's ship, with a cannon shot at his heels."

"From which the shot parted, by the rope giving way, as he sank into the water."

"Parted?"

"*Oui, monsieur;* so he told me; and thereupon he immediately rose to the surface and swam to the shore, while his less fortunate companion was instantly drowned."

"And how came you to be in his power? pardon my curiosity."

"It is most natural; I shall tell you, monsieur. Fearing that the province was to be overrun by your troops, we left our Chateau of Bourgneuf——"

"We, mademoiselle?"

"My aunt, Madame de Bourgneuf, and myself, to take shelter in the city of St. Malo; but our carriage arrived at St. Solidore too late last night, and Captain de Boisguiller, commandant of the redoubt at Cancalle——"

"Ah, that little redoubt cost us some trouble."

"Gave us his own residence. You know what ensued. Cannon shot fell through the roof of the house, on which my aunt, our servants, and I rushed forth into the streets, and were separated by a crowd of terrified fugitives. Ignorant alike whither to turn my steps, or where to seek shelter, while shells were bursting, flaming rockets and hand-grenades flying about in every direction, I rushed into a lonely alley, where I met a man who, by his attire, seemed to be one of our Breton peasantry—a woodcutter; but ah, *mon Dieu!* he proved to be that wretch, Theophile Hautois. Politely enough he offered to conduct me to a place of safety, and led me from St. Solidore, away out into the fields, where the country was open and lonely. There he spoke of love, and attempted to kiss and caress me; but I resisted, though sinking with terror, and struck him in the face with my clenched hand. Then he grew enraged, and tying my wrists, dragged me into that mulberry grove, where heaven surely sent you to my rescue."

"I am, indeed, most fortunate in having

been of such service to you, mademoiselle; and I shall ever remember with pride that I have seen and had the honour of speaking with a daughter of the great Marshal de Broglie, the hero of Sangerhausen."

She bowed and coloured with pleasure; but when the sound of wheels was heard, she clasped her hands and exclaimed—

"*Ah, mon Dieu,* how fortunate! Now, my kind friend, you shall be relieved of all further trouble with me, for here comes good and kind Father Celestine, le Curé of St. Solidore."

While she spoke, a *désobligeant* (as those small chaises which hold only one person are not incorrectly named in France) was driven rapidly along the road; but the driver pulled up when my companion called to him by name:

"Jacquot—Jacquot Tricot—where is M. le Curé?"

"Here, mademoiselle. Oh, *Clementissime Jesu!* what has happened? how are you here?—who is this man?—why in such company? and who has dared—what has he done to you? my dear child, Jacqueline, what is the meaning of all this?" cried an old gentleman, all in a breath, as he opened the door of the *désobligeant* and sprang agilely out. As he approached us, hat in hand, and bowing low at every pace, I could see that he was a fine looking old man—a priest, evidently, as he wore a black silk soutan, with at least fifty little buttons in front; he wore also a tippet and small gold cross, and had his white hair tied behind by a black ribbon. His pale countenance was mdil and pleasing, though he surveyed me with an expression of eye which evinced that he had no particular desire to cultivate *my* acquaintance; and maitre Jacquot from his box regarded me with undisguised animosity and alarm.

"Ah, dearest Père Celestine," said the young lady, clasping his proffered hand between both of hers, "I have been saved from great peril by this kind soldier; but take me away with you—oh, take me away —and I shall tell you all about it."

"Kind—ha—hum. *Monsieur le Soldat*, I thank you," said the Curé, making a bow so profound, that a cloud of hair-powder flew about his head, and his little cocked hat, which he was too polite to assume before a lady, swept the road in his right hand; "from my soul I thank you, for Mademoiselle Jacqueline is my dearest child."

"Have I the honour of addressing——" I began, for this phraseology bewildered me.

"Le Père Celestine," said Mademoiselle

de Broglie; "so I am now in perfect safety, thanks to your kindness and courage, monsieur; and now permit me to offer you that reward which any soldier may accept without reproach."

She drew a ring from her finger, and placed it in my hand, saying, with a bright coquettish smile—

"There is a language of precious stones, as well as of beautiful flowers, and if learned in such matters, you will know what this gem is significant of."

The old clergyman waved his hat, and laughed with great good humour, while the graceful girl bowed to me again and again as he handed her into the *dés-obligeant* and shut the door. The Curé then placed his hat on his head, for the first time during our interview, and with true French gallantry sprang on the narrow footboard behind his little carriage, which was rapidly driven off, Jacquot evincing, by his lavish use of the whip, his desire to place as great a distance as possible between himself and me.

The whole affair was like a dream. I placed the ring on my smallest finger, and thought with delight of the lovely little hand from which it had just been drawn. I gave a lingering glance after the fast-retreating *désobligeant*, which was bowling along the road towards the ruined village of St. Solidore, and then, springing into my saddle, galloped in the direction of our camp, the white tents of which were shining in the rising sun, as they dotted the southern slope of the hills of Paramé.

The stone was a fine emerald.

"Of what is it significant?" thought I, remembering her words and her charming smile.

Charters, whom I met with three

mounted Greys, coming in search of me, by order of the adjutant, told me that, "according to an old superstition, the emerald was supposed to ensure success in love."

Be that as it may, this gift of Jacqueline de Broglie has yet an important part to play in the story of my adventures.

END OF VOL. I.

LONDON:
SAVILL AND EDWARDS, PRINTERS,
CHANDOS-STREET.

www.ingramcontent.com/pod-product-compliance
Lightning Source LLC
Chambersburg PA
CBHW021214270326
41929CB00010B/1120
9783744776189